Decision-Making and the Information System

Advances in Information Systems Set

coordinated by
Camille Rosenthal-Sabroux

Volume 3

Decision-Making and the Information System

Maryse Salles

WILEY

First published 2015 in Great Britain and the United States by ISTE Ltd and John Wiley & Sons, Inc.

ISTE Ltd
27-37 St George's Road
London SW19 4EU
UK

www.iste.co.uk

John Wiley & Sons, Inc.
111 River Street
Hoboken, NJ 07030
USA

www.wiley.com

Library of Congress Control Number: 2015940035

British Library Cataloguing-in-Publication Data
A CIP record for this book is available from the British Library
ISBN 978-1-84821-753-9

Contents

Introduction

The purpose of this book is to question the relationships involved in decision-making and the systems designed to support it: decision support systems (DSS). The focus is on how these systems are engineered; the aim is not to provide a detailed description of various methods or technical tools, but rather to stop and think about the questions to be asked throughout the engineering process and, in particular, about the impact designers' choices have on these systems.

This involves identifying the elements of the problem of decision support systems engineering: the main objects and dimensions to be considered and the relationships they involve, issues at the levels of the decision-maker, the organization (and even the society), the general approach to which to subscribe and so on.

When mentioning the objects and dimensions of decision support systems engineering [SPR 82] highlight that "it is important to recall that the overall system is the decision-making system, consisting of *manager/user*, who uses a *DSS* to confront a *[decision-related] task* in an *organizational environment*" [our emphasis].

This book is organized into four chapters. The first two chapters deal with these four objects (manager/user, decision-making task, organizational environment, DSS), whereas the last two chapters will discuss the relationships of influence they involve and the need to manage them. A short presentation of these chapters is given below.[1]

The core of decision support: decision-making, the decision-maker and the organization

Chapter 1 will focus on *decision-making*, on the process implemented by the decision-maker, on its position in the life of an organization (three of the components of the aforementioned global decision-making system) and on the latter's environment.

"To decide" means to determine what we are going to do. The verb "decide" is derived from the Latin *decidere*, which literally means to slice, cut or reduce.

Deciding therefore means making a choice (which implies that there are several possible options) and then being *responsible* for this selection. The author believes that decision-making, which cannot be detached from responsibility, is the prerogative of mankind and of mankind alone. To use this term for digital objects (in the broadest sense of programs, agents, robots, etc.) is a misuse of language, which is certainly worth questioning.

There are two main different and opposing approaches to decision-making:

– the first approach, often called normative decision theory, is based on rationality and aims to optimize decision-making by identifying for each situation a utility function that must be maximized [LÉV 89]. The problem is, therefore, considered as given. It should be pointed out that if we agree with the idea of decision-making described above, normative decision theory is not really decision-making at all, as its aim is to produce one (and only one) optimal selection, meaning that all the decision-maker has to do is confirm this choice;

---

1 Chapters 1 and 2 are partially inspired by Salles [SAL 13].

– the second approach, coming from the work of Simon [SIM 60, SIM 77], takes into account the complexity of decision-making situations and the limited rationality of the decision-maker. Alcaras [ALC 04] called this the theory of decision engineering, in the sense that its object is the global decision-making process (including the definition of the problem) and not only its result, as normative theory suggests. This book explains this approach.

The focus will then shift to the *decision-maker*, who is considered throughout the decision-making process which they use to realize their task, as modeled by Simon [SIM 60] and completed by other authors. The importance of the first phase of the process – i.e. defining the problem – is emphasized. For unstructured or wicked problems, this phase determines the decision made.

Decision-making is an integral part of the life of organizations. As complex systems immersed in moving environments, they must indeed be managed: their principal missions need to be defined, their objectives need to be set, the achievement of the latter should be accompanied and then evaluated and corrective measures are to be decided. The chapter addresses the *organizational environment* of decision-making by modeling how the system (the organization) is managed. The components of the model are described, alongside the dynamics linking them.

Organizational and extra-organizational environments have gone through significant changes over the past 50 years, which have a direct impact on decision-making and the requirements with regard to decision support, in particular for high-level decisions (strategic and, to a lesser extent, tactical). An analysis of these evolutions will conclude the first chapter.

Information systems (IS) and decision support systems

The fourth component of the global decision-making system according to Sprague and Carlson [SPR 82], the *decision support system*, is the subject of Chapter 2.

Originating from systems theory, which considers a business, a state service or a territorial collectivity a complex system, the concept of the IS was created in the early 1970s to differentiate it from the information technology (IT) system. Le Moigne [LEM 73] defines the IS of an organization as a set of significant, formal or informal symbols circulating inside it, assimilating it therefore to a language, i.e. a capacity to take account of the "real" (and/or to construct it) in a way that can be shared by a given community. More recent definitions reinforce this idea by identifying the IS as "a set of social players who memorize and transform representations (...)" [REI 02]. An IS is therefore presented as a system that formalizes representations and that makes these formalizations operational and accessible (and active) through specific codifications.

The IS, which cannot be dissociated from the organization to which it belongs and its environment [MÉL 79], has two main functions [LEM 77]. The first function is to formalize the shared representations that are required for the system to realize its mission, i.e. to produce in the broad sense (Le Moigne refers to this part as the operating system). The second function is to produce representations of the system and its environment which are necessary for managing it (in Le Moigne's terminology, the decision system). These two types of representations overlap only in part.

From an early stage, research has focused on the decision support function of IS [GOR 71], greatly preceding the arrival of specific IT tools.

The IT or digital system is a subset of the IS and it ensures the automatable part of these two functions. From their inception, IT systems have focused on assisting the operating system and, since the 1980s, have made the move toward support for the decision systems to constitute a specific activity sector – business intelligence – and specific tools – DSS.

Chapter 2 will provide an overview of the main definitions of DSS and their evolution through history. Several typologies used to categorize them will then be presented.

A brief history of research in the domain will be presented, showing that after a first period of rich and open research when the problems of the domain were posed in a multidisciplinary approach, a second phase occurred almost totally focusing on technical aspects, and then, faced with certain failings of DSS, in a third period, a new interest arose for decision-makers and their needs, and the role of the decision within organizations. The thundering arrival of Big Data could shift the focus of the domain once again toward technology, as encouraged by the thriving sector of business intelligence.

The chapter will then discuss DSS design with a focus on the requirement engineering phase. This phase determines the organizational objective of the DSS and its content, as well as the type of interaction at work between the decision-maker and the system. It is, moreover, a phase of exchange between all the players in the project and, as such, is essential to ensure the DSS matches its requirements and to evaluate its impact on stakeholders as a whole, the latter being a central point for us.

The impact of the DSS on decision-making and related risks

Chapter 3 will discuss the *relationships* DSS have with the three other objects in the global decision-making system and, in particular, the impact of these tools on the decision-making process.

Research into decision-making has shown the importance of the problem formulation phase [PAR 08], on the one hand, and the determining role mental representations (world views, values, beliefs, etc.) play in this formulation [MIT 97], on the other hand.

First, the chapter will attempt to question the "neutrality" of management tools in general [BER 83] and IS and IT systems (including DSS) in particular. By their very nature, which is to formalize the representations (and thus reduce the complexity of the real), and through their role, which is to make these representations shareable and shared between the players in an organization, the IS produce performative effects. Some tools (e.g. indicators), which constitute equivalents of the organization's operation, evaluate the latter at the cost of drastically reducing the real.

In the computerized part of IS – IT system – the effects of reducing the real, and performativity, are further accentuated. In view of these effects, we will question the role of DSS in decision-making, in general, and then for the specific type of DSS that constitute Big Data.

The active role of DSS in decision-making will then lead us to consider the risks related to their use. A number of types of risks will be studied: data or processing errors, the risk of confusing the real and its digital representation, the risk of feedback which the performativity of these systems involves and the risk of the loss of diversity in the way problems being asked in organizations are tackled. The biggest danger, which is a result of the aforementioned risks, is that of limiting organizations' *ability to innovate*, as innovation requires new ideas about the organization, its environment and the organization's connection with the latter to be developed. Inscribing in IT system and DSS a unique world view, which is highly restrictive yet undebated (as it is for the most part implicit), also poses the problem of the democracy in the life of organizations.

Finally, the uncontrolled quest for predictive and even prescriptive decision support (which would replace the decision-maker) results, via certain aspects of Big Data and its present or future uses, in disturbing problems at the epistemological and democratic levels. A general and worrying picture is being drawn in the discourse of a number of promoters of Big Data [AND 08, MAY 13]: the refusal of the irreducible diversity of the real, the denial of the necessary complexity of human thought and the devaluation of experience as a primary source of knowledge.

Faced with the immense potential offered by authentic decision support, but also with the real risk of technology that would occultly guide human decision-making, it seems absolutely vital to question the way DSS are built. Their designers, all the stakeholders involved, have a *responsibility* with regard to how DSS are used and to the consequences of any decisions made with their support. By "responsibility", we mean moral responsibility (and not merely accountability), i.e. a person must hold his/her actions up to his/her conscience and *ethical* values.

Toward ethical DSS design

The recognization of this moral responsibility – which is also economic and social – and its accompaniment are the subject of the fourth and final chapter of this book.

This question, which, strangely, is mentioned very seldom in the literature in the domains of IT systems and DSS, falls into the category of *computer ethics*. Although there has been a concern about ethics since the dawn of cybernetics [WIE 48], computer ethics remains largely absent from IT research and teaching.

A quick state of the art about computer ethics, in general, the ethical theories on which it is based, its objects, the list of values supported, and also its production with regard to IT systems design methods, therefore seemed necessary. From this review, it can be considered that research into computer ethics mostly remains a topic for philosophers, and that research focuses a great deal on topics concerning the individuals (and not organizations) and their use of IT systems in their private life (and not in their professional life). Privacy, accessibility, transparency and non-discrimination are, therefore, the most frequently defended values. With some rare exceptions [STA 10], economic and social questions are not discussed.

Although the ethics of decision-making has resulted in a significant volume of literature, in particular in medicine and in the domain of management sciences, the ethics of DSS remains largely unexplored, in keeping with the computer profession's indifference to ethical questions. Some researchers have got upset about this, such as Meredith and Arnott [MER 03], who note that it is "unfortunate that the ethics of decision support as a specific topic has received very little attention in comparison to the issues of privacy and other general IT ethics issues". The arrival of Big Data has, however, sparked a new interest in the consequences of its use on both individuals and (particularly public) organizations.

With regard to the aforementioned issues, particularly the limitation of decision-makers' and organizations' abilities by inscribing one single worldview in DSS, which are reinforced by the effects of feedback and the distance from the real, the ethical value we are looking to promote is *democracy*. For us, this involves producing DSS which meet the requirements of democracy, especially the ability to access multiple worldviews.

If we decide to consider the designers and all the stakeholders as morally, economically and socially responsible for how DSS are used, our position can only be upheld if this responsibility is assisted.

As such, we support the creation of *engineering of responsibility* and, with this aim, we will present a methodological tool: the doxai-principles-norms (DPN) model. This model unveils the chain starting with representations (worldviews) and ending with norms (the most operational level), passing through an intermediary level (the structuring principles). The model is destined to accompany the highest phase of engineering requirements – the analysis of early requirements – when the global aim of the future DSS is aligned with the overall objectives of the organization. This phase is essential as it sets the representations (about the organization, its players, objects, etc.), which will form the framework in which the features of the DSS and the ethical values to be integrated will be inscribed. An illustration of the DPN model will conclude this chapter.

Decision-Making

Introduction: decision-making, the central issue of decision support

In an engineering approach to decision support systems (DSS), the technical aspects, however complex, must never forget that *decision-making* is the central issue of decision support. This chapter will explore the different dimensions of decision-making so that we can understand its content, its *sense*.

It is worth reiterating that decision-making is the prerogative of mankind and that a "decision" made by a digital machine is *not* a decision (however, complex, it is nothing but the result of a line of calculations).

Every human being, in their personal and professional life and in their life as a citizen, is almost constantly making decisions of varying degrees of importance. To illustrate (basic) decision-making, let us consider the following: a pedestrian walking from one place to another will decide which route to take, during the journey they will choose which pavement to walk on, where and when to cross the road, how fast to walk, etc., until they decide to stop when they think they have arrived at their destination.

Similarly, decision-making is an integral part of the life of human organizations (authorities, enterprises, the State, etc.). Complex systems are immersed in moving environments, and they must indeed be managed. Managing takes various forms, but in the end it always results in individuals or groups making decisions. Enterprises must, for example, choose suppliers, organize production, set the price of products, define a client segment, redistribute the tasks of an absent worker, recruit employees and define the axes of research and development, and so on.

This book will focus on the decisions made within organizations, and not those made in individuals' private lives.

Section 1.1 will present two different and opposing approaches to decision-making. The first approach is based on a rational view of decision-making and aims to optimize the final choice. The second approach, taken from research by Simon [SIM 60, SIM 77], takes the limitations of the decision maker's rationality into account and seeks to help them make the most satisfactory decision for them.

In the domain of DSS, decision-making is understood in several dimensions, which can be split into two categories: the first category concerns the individuals making the decisions (the decision makers) and the second category concerns the methods and the roles of decision-making in the life of organizations.

Section 1.2 will focus on the decision maker (or a group of decision makers). First, the decision-making process modeled by Simon [SIM 60] will be studied. Given that the process is partially determined by the degree of formalization of the problems being asked to the decision maker, we will then discuss how decisions are structured (including the specific case of undefined or "wicked" problems). Some specificities of group decision-making will conclude this section.

This book discusses decision-making within organizations; section 1.3 will focus on the organizational context of decision-making. Organizations can be seen as complex systems. Systems theory has presented a management model, which we will describe in detail. Out of its components, indicators play a vital role. A definition of indicators will be provided and then a typology will be presented. We will then reflect on the distinction that must be drawn between decisions that have an impact on the definition of the management system and decisions that operate within the framework of this system (action decisions). The section will conclude with an important dimension of decision-making within organizations: the level of management (operational, tactical or strategic).

Organizations are immersed in an environment and they interact with it. It has often been said that this environment has been constantly changing for the past 20 years. Section 1.4 is dedicated to analyzing these changes and their impact on the content of decisions. The different dimensions of these changes will be studied with regard to organizations: their connection with the environment, establishing their boundaries and their needs in terms of the information system (IS). Public institutions and their evolution will specifically be discussed.

1.1. Normative theory versus engineering theory

Economics, management sciences and computer sciences are interested in decision support design (whichever forms these supports take). These areas have taken two main approaches to decision-making. The first approach, which we will call *normative* decision theory [ALC 04], mostly comes from economic sciences and is based on a rational view of decision-making (for more details, see [KAS 93]). Decision-making is assimilated to calculations determining the best possible action (i.e. optimum). This approach is based on what Simon [SIM 76] calls *substantive* rationality:

> Behavior is substantively rational when it is appropriate
> to the achievement of given goals within the limits
> imposed by given conditions and constraints.

Defining the pursued objectives, defining the problem the decision needs to solve, choosing the relevant perimeter, identifying the necessary information, etc., are seen as exogenous to the decision-making process and as *given*. Simon *et al.* [SIM 86] wrote the following about subjective expected utility (SEU):

SEU theory defines the conditions of perfect utility-maximizing rationality in a world of certainty or in a world in which the probability distributions of all relevant variables can be provided by the decision makers. (…) SEU theory deals only with decision making; it has nothing to say about how to frame problems, set goals, or develop new alternatives.

Lévine and Pomerol [LÉV 89] summarized the hypotheses based on normative theory as follows:

– all possible actions are identified before the start of the decision-making process;

– there is a total preorder for actions, which can be represented by an explicit utility function and can be given a mathematical expression;

– input (parameters and data) is digital and contains all useful information;

– the best decision is that which maximizes the utility function.

Normative decision theory has been undeniably successful for repetitive and well-defined problems, for which all the useful information is available. These situations most often correspond with operational decisions, rarely with tactical decisions and never with strategic decisions.

We can even question the *decisional* nature of the activities carried out in this context. For a decision maker, choosing the optimum, i.e. only accepting the best choice, is not really decision-making (which would imply a set of possible choices), but rather the ratification of what is essentially the result of a calculation. It should be noted that using normative theory to deal with strategic decision-making generates excessive risks of reducing complexity and losing diversity (this will be discussed in Chapter 3).

A large number of decision-making situations come out of the very restricted context of normative theory. These situations are characterized by the limitations of the decision maker's (substantive) rationality. These limitations are particularly visible in situations perceived to be *complex* by the decision maker.

Alcaras [ALC 11] shows that three types of factors contribute to this complexity, which he calls informational, teleological and computational, respectively:

– informational factors: information required for decision-making is difficult to define, collect or process in the time available;

– teleological factors: the end purpose pursued in decision-making is not always clear, nor shared by everyone involved in making the decision; consequently, the selection criteria are not very easy to set;

– computational factors: humans' computational skills are limited: attention span, calculation skills, short- and long-term memory, etc.

Following Simon, another approach was developed, which is based on *procedural* rationality rather than substantive rationality. The main focus shifted, therefore, from the result of the decision-making (which should "simply" be optimized) to the *process* of decision-making, which concludes not when the optimum is achieved, but according to the criterion of *satisficing* (see section 1.2.2). This position, which focuses first and foremost on the way in which decisions are made (including defining the problem), was called the theory of decision engineering by Alcaras [ALC 04]. This book subscribes to this approach.

1.2. The decision process

1.2.1. *Simon's IDC model*

The domain of decision support has, since its inception, been aligned with Simon's work and has, therefore, focused on the process an individual develops to make a decision.

Simon identifies the decision process as a problem-solving process. He focuses not on the choice but on the whole process [SIM 60] and takes issue with focusing on this one "final moment".

[They] ignore the whole lengthy, complex process of alerting, exploring, and analyzing that precedes that final moment. In treating decision making as synonymous with managing, I shall be referring not merely to the final act of choice among alternatives, but rather to the whole process of decision.

To describe this process, Simon [SIM 60, SIM 77] proposes a generic three-phase structure known as the intelligence, design, choice (IDC) process, which is close, as the author specifies, to the problem-solving approach described by Dewey [DEW 10]:

The first phase of the decision-making process – searching the environment for conditions calling for a decision – I shall call intelligence activity (borrowing the military meaning of intelligence). The second phase – inventing, developing, and analyzing possible courses of action – I shall call design activity. The third phase – selecting course of action from those available – I shall call choice activity [SIM 77].

The fourth and final phase (review), which evaluates the relevance of the choices made in the previous phases, is often omitted; yet, it enables a new decision-making process to be launched.

"The fourth phase – assessing past choices, I shall call review activity".

Simon stresses that the transition from one phase to another is not really sequential, but rather that it involves an iterative or even recursive operation, where each phase is itself a decision process:

Generally speaking, intelligence activity precedes design, and design activity precedes choice. The cycle of phases is, however, far more complex than the sequence suggests. Each phase in making a particular decision is itself a complex decision making process. The design phase, for example, may call for new intelligence activities; problems at any given level generate sub problems that in turn have their own intelligence, design and choice phases, and so on. There are wheels within wheels.

It should be noted that this process can be likened to spiral models [BOE 88] in software engineering and, more broadly, to agile methods (rapid application devepmenlot (RAD), dynamic systems development method (DSDM), extreme programming (XP), etc.).

The IDC model remains a point of reference for weakly structured or unstructured decisions (see section 1.2.3), notably in the domain of DSS design [POM 05].

1.2.1.1. *A few words on the intelligence phase*

The intelligence phase places the beginning of the decision process very upstream and starts with the understanding that a decision must be taken. It continues by constructing a representation of the perceived problem. Simon *et al.* [SIM 86] insist on the importance of this phase, which they believe is not well understood:

> The very first steps in the problem-solving process are the least understood. What brings (and should bring) problems to the head of the agenda? And when a problem is identified, how can it be represented in a way that facilitates its solution?

1.2.1.2. *The satisficing principle*

In opposition to normative theory, which considers decision-making to be searching for an optimum, Simon proposes the satisficing principle. The term *satisficing* is a portmanteau combining *to satisfy* with *to suffice*.

This principle describes decision makers' behavior when faced with a situation for which developing an optimal solution using a set of constraints (related to time, cost, availability of the information, the attention span of the decision maker, their limited rationality, etc.) is considered impossible. A decision is assessed against the satisficing criteria of the individual decision maker and their aspiration level for the decision in question:

> Stop searching as soon as you have found an alternative
> that meets your aspiration level [SIM 79].

Contrary to approaches aimed at optimization, not all of the alternatives are explored: the decision maker stops when they judge the solution to be *satisficing*, i.e. good enough. Over this decision-making process, the satisficing principle governs not only the stopping of the process at a final choice, but also all the internal decisions involved in the process (the "wheels within wheels"): stopping or returning to a task within a phase, moving onto the next phase, going back to the previous phase and so on.

1.2.2. *Supplementing the IDC model*

Simon's model has been supplemented by other authors such as Mintzberg *et al.* [MIN 76], who present a process model for unstructured decisions, in particular strategic decisions. This model, built from a field study on 25 strategic decision-making processes, has three stages, which the authors specify "resemble Simon's trichotomy", although it uses other terms ("identification", "development" and "selection"). An in-depth analysis led the authors to identify seven procedures within the three stages, which are supplemented by support procedures:

– the identification stage, composed of two routines: recognizing the need to make a decision and diagnosing the situation;

– the development stage, which constructs one or more solutions to the problem identified in the first phase. It uses two procedures: research to try to find ready-made solutions (for example, by benchmarking[1]) and design to create specific solutions or modify the ready-made solutions;

– selection, the last stage of the process, which is, as the authors commented, closely linked to the previous phase:

---

1 *Benchmarking* should be understood here in the broadest sense: a comparison not only of products, but also of methods, processes and even strategic choices. These studies can be conducted within one activity sector or outside reference in a specific activity.

> because the development phase frequently involves factoring one decision into a series of subdecisions, each requiring at least one selection step, one decision process could involve a great number of selection steps [...] [MIN 76].

The iterative character of the decision process highlighted by Simon is confirmed once again. Furthermore, the authors query the sequential character and the clear demarcation of the three procedures, which normative decision theory recognizes in the last phase: the determination of selection criteria, evaluating alternatives with these criteria and selection. Mintzberg *et al.* [MIN 76] suggest describing the selection phase as an iterative process, which progressively analyses the alternatives in more detail over three procedures: filtering realizable alternatives to reduce the number of alternatives, evaluation-choice to analyze the remaining alternatives and choosing a line of action and, if required by the position of the decision maker, authorization so that the chosen line of action can be ratified by a superior.

The [MIN 76] model both corroborates Simon's model and improves the description of its different phases.

The weighting of the steps in the process (unveiled by the study) gives importance to the aspects of constructing the representation of the problem (recognizing the need to make a decision, diagnosing the situation and so on), which corresponds to Simon's intelligence phase. Like the latter, Mintzberg *et al.* [MIN 76] consider this phase to be a major issue, particularly if the very real risk of "solving the wrong problems precisely" is to be avoided [MIT 10].

Moreover, the description of the large majority of procedures focuses on their implicit, intuitive, not very rational, unrational or even *a posteriori* rationalized character. The importance of constructing the representation of the problem, such as the implicit and non-analytical character of the procedures, results in the central role of the mental models, representations and worldviews in decision-making to be recognized. We will return to this question later, particularly in Chapter 3.

1.2.3. *Structuring decisions*

The way the decision process described above is applied differs depending on the characteristics of the decisions concerned. Among the characteristics, the decision's degree of formalization is the subject of great interest in the domain of decision support. It can be described from the perspective either of the decision makers – we thus talk about structuring decisions – or of the organization – related to the standardization of decisions (see section 1.3.8).

In his decision process model, Simon draws a distinction between programmed and non-programmed decisions. He specifies that these two categories are not two disconnected units but rather are the extreme ends of a *continuum*. Programmed decisions are described as repetitive decisions, for which the organization or the decision maker has defined a clear procedure. Conversely, non-programmed decisions are for the most part new and there are no ready-made methods to deal with them. This is the case for previously unseen problems or when their structure is complex and/or changing, or when their potential impact is so great that it is worth paying them special attention.

Gorry and Scott-Morton [GOR 71] return to these categories to characterize decisions, but they rename them *structured* and *unstructured* decisions as the term "programmed" expresses too great a dependence on information technology (IT) tools. We will use their terms (structured and unstructured decisions) in this book. As will be seen in Chapter 2, DSS are intended to support weakly structured or unstructured decisions.

1.2.4. *Defined problems (tame) and undefined problems (wicked)*

The categories of structured and unstructured decisions are similar to the notion of defined (tame) and undefined (wicked) problems. The latter originally appeared in the domain of public policy [RIT 73], but today some researchers apply the terms more broadly, particularly in business management. Conklin [CON 01] describes defined problems (A tame problem) as having the following traits:

– has a relatively well-defined and stable problem statement;

– has a definite stopping point, i.e. we know when the solution is reached;

– has a solution which can be objectively evaluated as being right or wrong;

– belongs to a class of similar problems which can be solved in a similar manner;

– has solutions which can be easily tried and abandoned;

– comes with a limited set of alternative solutions.

In contrast, he summarizes the characteristics of undefined problems (wicked problem) as:

– the problem is not understood until after the formulation of a solution;

– wicked problems have no stopping rule;

– solutions to wicked problems are not right or wrong;

– every wicked problem is essentially novel and unique;

– every solution to a wicked problem is a "one shot operation";

– wicked problems have no given alternative solutions.

Stressing the crucial character of the representation of the problem, Ritchey [RIT 05] adds:

"The existence of a discrepancy representing a wicked problem can be explained in numerous ways. The choice of explanation determines the nature of the problem's resolution".

It should be noted that decisions about undefined problems are mostly unstructured decisions.

1.2.5. *Group decision-making*

Originally, the IDC model was built to represent an individual's decision process. Collective decision-making complicates this process in several ways. How groups function when making decisions collectively is the subject of a large amount of research across different disciplines, in particularly psychology and decision support.

In psychology, group functioning has notably been studied by Lewin [LEW 47], the founder of dynamic group theory, and in France by Anzieu and Martin [ANZ 86] and Mucchielli [MUC 13]. Research on groups focuses on their cohesion, power and influence relationships, locomotion methods (changes to the group's psychological state) and the ways in which decisions are made.

In the domain of DSS, Marakas [MAR 03] identifies five components that have an impact on group decision-making:

– the structure of the group, which is determined by the number of people in the group as well as the existing relationships between group members (hierarchical group, group of pairs, informal group, etc.);

– the different roles existing within the group and their definitive (a person holds one position which does not change) or evolutionary (a person can change their position) character;

– the processes implemented by the group and their degree of formalization and explicitation;

– the style of the group and, specifically, the type of management practiced by the group leader (authoritative, participatory, democratic, etc., management);

– the group's standards, which relate to representations and, more broadly, to the beliefs shared by the group, as well as to the rules set by the organization.

The question of shared representations (those which the group had at the beginning and those which it must build to reach a joint decision) is therefore, once again, essential.

1.3. Decision-making within the organization

We have already discussed decision-making from the perspective of one or a number of decision makers; in this section, we will focus on decision-making in its *organizational context*.

1.3.1. *Managing a complex system*

This section will briefly describe the main components of the management of a complex system, drawing inspiration from systems theory and more specifically research by Mélèse [MÉL 72], whose management model is still incredibly robust.

Henceforth, the unit considered in analysis will be called the *system*. An enterprise, a State service and an authority can, therefore, all be seen as systems, as can one of their branches or one of the services of a branch.

Systems theory divides all types of systems into three subsystems (which for reasons of simplicity we will call "systems"): the management system (which some authors call the "decision system"), the production system (in a wider sense) and the IS. To clearly identify decisions made from the general framework in which they are made, we will use the term "management system" (rather than decision system).

The *management system*:

– sets objectives (effectiveness, costs, etc.), in respect of which the mission must be carried out, and the resources devoted to it ;

– transmits them to the production system (in a comprehensible, realizable and controllable way);

– checks the stage of completion of the objectives and the degree to which the constraints have been respected (which involves, via feedback, a new management cycle: decision-making to correct the action of the production system).

The *production system* definitively realizes the mission of the system following the conditions (objectives, constraints and financial resources) set by the management system.

The *IS* conveys representations of the organization about itself, its environment and about the relationships it has with the latter.

An enterprise's IS is perceptible through, for instance:

– *the types of entities which are decisive for the operation of the enterprise (enterprise activities, clients, products, suppliers, market segments, categories of client, families of products, etc.) or its development and even survival (competitors, partners, the enterprise's key technologies, categories of consumers, etc.); in territorial authorities, these entities can be: the population, the territory and resources (financial, staff, real-estate patrimony, movable heritage, etc.);*

– *characteristics considered relevant for describing these entities (a client is described with a reference number, their business name, address, the names of the contact persons, the normal delivery address and the billing address; it is possible to find out the year of their first order, the total revenue from this client, the list of payments, etc.);*

– *stables names (the list of products sold by the enterprise, its hierarchy and the list of different departments and services it contains, the accounting system and its accounts, etc.);*

– *formalized procedures and rules (purchasing procedures, rules for calculating discounts, security rules, confidentiality levels, etc.), etc.*

The IS expresses the representations needed by the production system for the mission to be realized, as well as those required for management. These two types of representation overlap only in part.

For instance, though the aforementioned information describing a client is useful for billing or contact (about a sale) purposes, it cannot help the user interpret information showing that revenue from this client has dropped nor help him or her determine which decisions to take to rectify the situation.

Another example: a region can distribute assistance to enterprises and use an IS to manage the action (application file including the name of the enterprise, its activity code, its revenue, its workforce, etc.; attribution procedures and; system for managing budgets), however, the information that is collected and processed cannot manage territorial economic development policies. Management may require the following, for example, to be known: the current skills of the enterprise and the skills it intends to develop, the partnerships it has sealed with other players and the sectors in which it is likely to intervene, etc.

It is important to note that it is through the (unique) representation of the real available in the IS, and particularly in its digital part, that the management is performed. Entities types, entities, characteristics and dimensions that are absent from the IS will, therefore, not be taken into account during management. It should be noted that data mining techniques only partially compensate for these absences, in particular at the levels of tactical and specifically strategic management. This includes Big Data, which will be discussed in Chapters 2 and 3.

1.3.2. *The main components of the management system*

The main components of the management system are shown in Figure 1.1 and are briefly described below. The components are numbered as they are in the diagram.

1.3.2.1. *The mission of the system*

The first element, which is common to the system in question as a whole is its *mission,* i.e. the system's purpose, the reason it exists. The mission is often expressed as an end purpose, which according to Mélèse is "the representation a group built of the system missions, in very general rather than operational terms".

The mission of enterprise X is to produce and sell airplanes.

The mission of region Y is to enable inhabitants in the territory to live harmoniously via sustainable development.

It should be noted that the definition of the system's mission can vary, and sometimes a great deal, within the organization in question from one type of stakeholder, group or person to another. Changes in the economic environment, which will be described later, have often profoundly changed the definition of an enterprise's mission. In the current economic situation, one of the ways in which particularly large enterprises have changed is that their mission and objective or method have been reversed.

The mission of enterprise X, which was to produce products Z with the objective (among others) of increasing share value, has evolved, by financialization strategies, into a mission to increase share value by the method (among others) of producing products Z.

1.3.2.2. The system of objectives

Three levels of expressing the objectives can be identified according to their degree of precision:

– the end purpose or mission of the system (see above);

– goals, which realize the end purpose by breaking them down into operational components;

– objectives, which specify the goals via evaluation criteria along with a level that must be met and a time horizon.

All these end purposes/goals/objectives constitute the *system of objectives* as defined by Mélèse [MÉL 72].

NB: the numbers at the end of the following section titles refer to elements in the diagram below (Figure 1.1).

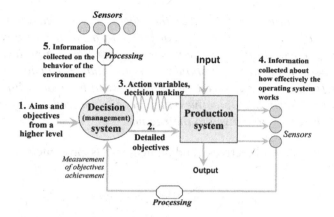

Figure 1.1. *Model for managing an organization (inspired by [MÉL 72]*

1.3.2.3. *Goals and objectives coming from a higher level (1)*

Objectives (and constraints) are imposed on the manager from a higher level.

For commercial managers, the higher level is the CEO. The CEO is in turn given goals and constraints from the board of directors. And finally, the expectations of financial markets, national or international regulations and countries' cultures provide the (sometimes implicit) constraints and objectives that are imposed on the board of directors.

1.3.2.4. *Detailed objectives (2)*

Managers deliver the objectives given to them from a higher level by adapting and breaking them down so that they are achievable, their achievement can be verified and they can be understood by the production system being managed.

Transposing the objectives received from a higher level is a major task for decision makers: it must enable them to improve their ability to control their production system and consequently, meet objectives by breaking them down into smaller objectives (in accordance with the potentially highly varied dimensions).

A commercial manager is given the objective of increasing revenue by 10% in a year. This objective can be broken down into a revenue objective per month, type of client or any other dimension devised by the commercial manager. It should be noted that a decision maker's skill can (in part) be measured by their ability to innovate with regard to breaking down the objectives they receive in order to form the detailed objectives to convey to their teams.

A typology of objectives (and indicators) is presented in section 1.3.4.

1.3.2.5. *Action variables and decision-making (3)*

Action variables relate to the options the decision maker has within the limits of the *decision-making latitudes* that have been imposed on him or her (e.g. the option to recruit or not to recruit, to use a budget freely or not freely, to change the way prices are set, services are organized, etc.).

Within the framework of these decision-making latitudes, the decision maker makes *effective decisions*, which are then implemented (employing workers, allocating a budget to an action, commissioning research, reorganizing the service, etc.).

The decision maker uses these action variables, which correspond to effective decision-making, to rectify the functioning of the production system to optimize the achievement of objectives in the short or medium term.

In the aforementioned example – to meet the objective of a rise in revenue – the commercial manager might decide to put a product on promotion, and/or change its packaging, and/or change the composition of the commercial teams so as to strengthen the action for certain client segments, etc.

1.3.2.6. *Sensors and indicators measuring the functioning of the production system (4)*

These sensors provide information about how the production system and its immediate environment work. They allow the production of indicators that will measure the achievement of the objectives set by the higher level (No. 1 in the diagram), as well as that of internal objectives (No. 2) set by the manager.

In the previous example, the indicator of the objective is clearly the total revenue achieved and its progress, but additional indicators are also required to measure whether detailed objectives have been met (revenue per type of product, client segment, sales advisor, etc.).

1.3.2.7. Sensors and indicators measuring the environment (5)

The aforementioned sensors often need to be supplemented with measurements of the broader environment so that predictions of future evolutions can be improved and, where necessary, some objectives can be redefined.

In our example, information about the environment may relate to competitors' (with the same type of products) revenue, competitors' current and future new products, the financial situation of important clients, new consumer behaviors, regulations being studied at the European level, etc.

1.3.2.8. Conclusion

Various research and applied research projects have testified the very high operationality of this simple model. For illustration purposes, decision supports can be categorized according to the components of this model: support to define objectives, support to break them down, support to understand the state of the production system, support to interpret the environment and support to choose an action variable (i.e. support to make decisions in the current sense of the term).

From our perspective, this model also has a major benefit: it draws a distinction between decisions that define the management system and decisions that result in real actions (we will return to this point in section 1.3.5).

1.3.3. *Indicator, index and information useful to the decision maker*

Figure 1.2 shows the relationships we establish between the notions of the indicator, the index and the information useful to the decision maker, which will be presented in this section.

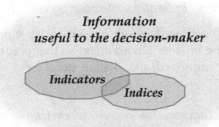

Figure 1.2. *Information, indicators and indices*

1.3.3.1. *Indicator*

The majority of existing definitions consider an indicator to be a direct or calculated measurement which is expressed either quantitatively or quantifiably. These numerous definitions mostly differ according to the degree of restriction of what an indicator helps assess.

An indicator can, therefore, measure the achievement of a given objective and is, as such, a key performance indicator (KPI). In addition to measuring performance, *indicator* also designates "any significant, relevant or irrelevant measurement used to assess results, the use of resources, the stage of work progress or the external context" [SCT 03].

For Fernandez [FER 05], the notion of indicator is extensive: it is "a piece of information or a set of information that help the decision-maker assess the situation".

We would like to put forward a more restricted definition of an indicator: *an indicator is a piece of formalized information which is produced regularly and which measures the realization of an action or the achievement of an objective.*

An indicator is, therefore, necessarily linked either to an action variable (i.e. the concrete implementation of a decision) or an objective (according to the management model presented above).

1.3.3.2. Index

In addition to the notion of indicators, we would like to put forward that of indices: *a piece of formalized information (a measurement) that is not directly linked to an objective or to an action variable will be called an index (and not an indicator); an index is either a one-off or a regular measurement.*

An index, therefore, focuses on:

– either an subject for which an objective cannot be set (for instance, an element of the environment that cannot be controlled: competitors' performance, the rate of change, the availability of rare raw materials, the socio-professional distribution of a population, etc.);

– or an subject that we have not, or have not yet, decided to control (for example, the numbers of a rare species of amphibians).

An index (either one-off or regular) can be used to help build the representation of a problem by taking stock of the existing situation.

It should be noted that this type of index may become an indicator if the organization sets an objective intended to change the situation and thus the value of the index. In the context of territorial economic development policies, a territorial authority can, for instance, use an index measuring the employment rate of young graduates to build a representation of the economic situation of the territory. It can subsequently create a policy whose objective is to increase the rate of employment in this category. The measurement, therefore, becomes an indicator of the achievement of this objective.

Another example is an enterprise which has production problems (for instance, the number of faulty products is too high). To identify the cause of the problem, measurements can be taken at different points in the process. Like in the previous example, one or more indices may become indicators if, for instance, a quality objective is set for a certain section of the production process.

1.3.3.3. *Information useful to the decision maker*

To gain an understanding of this notion, let us look at Mélèse's definition [MÉL 79] of information[2]:

> For a human being (or an automaton) any signal, message or perception that has an impact on their behavior or cognitive state is information.

Information useful to a decision maker will, therefore, for us be: *any signal, message or perception that has an impact on the behavior or the cognitive state of the decision maker and helps them with the various phases of their decision process.*

Information useful to a decision maker can be formal or informal, oral or on hardware support (including digital), text or not text, verified or unverified, etc. According to the definition we have put forward, indicators or indices are specific cases of information useful to a decision maker.

1.3.4. *Typology of objectives and indicators*

The management model presented by Mélèse [MÉL 72], whose effectiveness is in part due to its simplicity, does not suggest a developed typology for objectives or indicators. Yet, it is important to have an elaborate understanding of these elements to get closer to the meaning of the decisions, while the DSS is being designed, in particular during the requirement engineering phase (see Chapter 2).

---

2 Chapter 3 (section 3.2.4.3.) draws a useful distinction between data, information and knowledge.

The Balanced Scorecard offers an advanced typology for objectives and their related indicators.

In their Balanced Scorecard method, Kaplan and Norton [KAP 96] consider that current indicators are no longer suited to modern enterprises as they reflect past performance (whereas future performance is most important). Moreover, they are mostly quantitative (whereas management also needs to be based on qualitative evaluation). To these *a posteriori* indicators, the authors propose adding qualitative indicators as well as indicators about the determinants of future performance (*a priori* indicators) which they organize into four perspectives. These perspectives relate to both objectives and indicators, which must measure their achievement. The first two perspectives are determinants of future performance (levers) and the last two perspectives are the results.

1.3.4.1. *Key structural levers: learning and growth perspective*

These objectives relate to the components of the organization, which determine the sustainable performance of the latter: people (skills and motivation), IS and methods for developing procedures.

1.3.4.2. *Key operational levers: internal business processes perspective*

The objectives of this perspective focus on the processes in which the organization must excel if it has to meet the objectives of its intermediary and final results (e.g. delivery times, quality of post-sales service, innovation, etc.).

1.3.4.3. *Intermediary results: customer perspective*

The objective of this perspective aims to improve the satisfaction of players who are in an environment close to that of the organization and who determine the final results. For Kaplan and Norton, this principally concerns the enterprise's clients.

1.3.4.4. *Final results: financial perspective*

Depending on the type of organization and its end purpose, these objectives tend to satisfy one or a number of stakeholders who may or may not be part of the organization. An enterprise can set itself financial objectives (aiming, for instance, to satisfy shareholders alone), which is, in fact, the definition Kaplan and Norton gave to this perspective. An enterprise may, however, set final goals which are not financial (for instance, enterprises operating in the social and solidarity economy). A territorial authority may set objectives that aim to improve the living conditions of all or part of the population in a territory.

1.3.4.5. *Strategy map linking the objectives*

There is a causal chain between the objectives of the different perspectives. The realization of objectives of the key structural levers enables performance at the level of key operational levels (key processes) to be improved, which, in turn, make it possible to achieve intermediary results, which are necessary if the final results are to be met (the final results being the organization's ultimate goal). Figure 1.3 shows an example of a causal chain in a (fictional) enterprise.

1.3.5. *Support to define the global management system or support for action decisions?*

Studying the literature in the domain of DSS shows that the difference between support to define the global management system (defining the system of objectives, decision-making latitudes, indicators, etc.) and support to make decisions resulting in an action[3] (decisions, therefore, made within the management system) is rarely explicitly established. This distinction is partially (though not specifically) dealt with in the description of the categories of management activities that are described in the following paragraph. The two problems overlap only in part.

---

3 For reasons of simplicity, we will, henceforth, call decisions whose direct result is an action: *action decisions*.

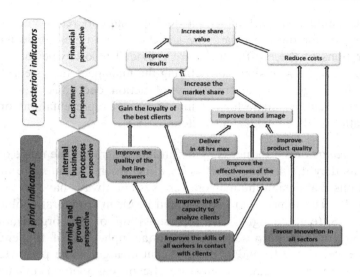

Figure 1.3. *Example of a strategy map for an enterprise*

Decisions that define the global management system determine the *framework* (objectives, constraints, resources, methods, measurement criteria, etc.) within which the action decisions are made. The former can be called meta-decisions as they are decisions concerning other decisions.

It is not always easy to draw a distinction between these two types of decisions. Simon [SIM 97] stresses that objectives, constraints and resources are positions that move and interchange over the course of the management process.

Moreover, defining the management system is not (as a superficial analysis may conclude) the prerogative of the senior management of an organization; rather, it operates on every level of the organization, i.e. for each subsystem comprising the global system (which could be an enterprise, territorial authority, a State service, etc.).

In the context of DSS design, we maintain that it is advisable to draw a distinction (as far as is possible) between decisions that define the management system and decisions that implement it.

We maintain in particular that decision support requirements are not, or not for the most part, the same for both types of decisions. Illustrations of these differences are provided below. The range and the frequency of decisions for defining the management system differ from the range and the frequency of action decisions. The same distinction can be made for the importance of representations or the evaluation of the management system.

The *range* of the former is by definition larger than the range of the latter as they define the *framework* within which the latter are made. Decisions that design the management system always have an impact on the IS. The impact can be great and result in structural evolutions of the IS (e.g. changing the representation of the organization's missions or end purpose resulting in an upheaval of the entities represented in the IS and/or a significant change of the perimeter of the IS). This impact can be (only) significant (e.g. methods evaluating the achievement of objectives are changed resulting in new columns being added to databases, indicator and dashboard calculations are changed throughout the organization as a whole). The impact may, however, be more limited (e.g. the decision-making latitudes of a manager are changed resulting in their dashboards being updated).

The *frequency* of decisions concerning the management system is irregular but generally lower and their range is larger, which goes hand in hand with limited reversibility. Action decisions (with the exception of some strategic decisions) are made at a faster pace than decisions that define the managing system (this pace may be very high for decisions made at the operational level).

Conceptual high-level *representations* (general views) produced by the organization (about itself, its missions, environment, position within the latter, the trajectory it will follow, etc.) have a significant impact on the organization of the management system (particularly objective setting). The design of a DSS intended to support the definition of the management system must, therefore, consider these representations, which are in part implicit and may vary or contradict each other within one organization. With regard to action decision-making support, the question of global representations is less important as these decisions (with the exception of strategic decisions) are made within an already-established system of objectives which express a set of representations. Naturally, the idea of the representation also applies when the decision maker *represents the problem* (the first phase of the decision-making process), although its range is noticeably reduced.

Our final example, the *evaluation* of the management system, is a complex, highly iterative and even recursive process. It is generally much more complex to assess the relevance of an objective to define the management system than it is to measure the effectiveness of an action helping to achieve an objective. The former are for the most part undefined problems (wicked problems): structuring them requires a great deal of effort and information – which is diverse and covers a broad spatial and temporal perimeter – to be collected and produced.

A further distinction concerns the type of decisions in terms of their subject, range and effect on the organization: in brief, their *management level*.

1.3.6. *Management levels*

The domain of management science has identified a number of categories of decisions based on their impact on the organization. Three levels are generally recognized. Borrowing military terminology, they are often known as the operational, tactical and strategic levels. The respective content of the three levels varies from one author to another, particularly with regard to the strategic level. That said, these categories have remained relatively stable over the past few decades.

Anthony [ANT 65] and then Ansoff [ANS 88] presented the categories of different types of decisions, which have since been very widely used. We will now present Ansoff's description of the levels. Ansoff mostly reiterates Anthony's categorization of levels 2 and 3, although his definition of strategic decisions deviates from Anthony's. For Anthony, the strategic level exclusively involves defining the management system, whereas for Ansoff it primarily involves defining the enterprise's relationship with its economic environment:

1) strategic decisions mostly concern the – external now rather than internal – activities of the enterprise and more specifically the choice of products they will produce and the markets where they will sell;

2) administrative decisions whose objective is to manage resources so as to obtain the best possible results. Administrative problems consist of, on the one hand, organizing the enterprise's structures (authority and responsibility relationships, work and information flows, communication channels and appointments) and, on the other hand, ensuring that resources are purchased and developed (namely, staff training, financing and purchasing equipment);

3) operational decisions' objective is to make the process of transforming resources as efficient as possible, in other words, to obtain maximum profits from current business.

Like many other authors, Ansoff specifies that the three categories are interdependent and complementary. The strategy requires operational measurements and the administrative structure must provide conditions to implement the strategy.

It is not always easy to fit a decision into one type of category. Mintzberg [MIN 94] remarks that:

> Decisions made for immediate purposes under short run pressures (…) can have the most long-range and strategic of consequences (…). Likewise, seemingly momentous "strategic" decisions can sometimes fizzle like a punctured ballon.

Systems theory [LEM 77] identifies several different types of ways a system evolves based on whether its relationship to the environment, and its end purpose and goals, is stable or changeable.

Four different ways of evolving a system have been identified, which can be interpreted as being either at the management level or at the decision level:

1) Regulation or stabilization (stable goal and stable environment);

The system is stable in a stable environment. The system of objectives and the organization as a whole remain unchanged. Only, the values of the adjustment parameters are changed to respond to slight disturbances in the environment. Regulation is an adaptation without memory, and therefore without learning.

Examples of regulation decisions: adjusting a machine when production changes, re-allocating resources in the short or very short term, dropping a price during negotiations between a salesperson and their client, deciding to deliver products to a client depending on their solvency and choosing an intern.

2) Functional adaptation (stable goals and changing environment);

Lasting modifications are identified in the environment. Management modifies the organization without calling into questions its end purpose or goals. This management level (like those below) involves learning.

Examples of functional adaptation decisions: reorganizing production into 2 × 8 h, reorganizing the workload of a commercial team (distributing prospects, the number of client visits, commercial documentation, etc.).

3) Structural adaptation (changing goals and stable environment);

The user recognizes that the environment is going through a stable period and decides to modify the end purpose of the system within certain limits. The system's inscription in its environment (mission) is modified, though it is not completely called into question.

Examples of structural adaptation: targeting a new type of client (e.g. private individuals for an enterprise who hitherto worked in business-to-business), innovative technology in the production process, launching a new product and changing pricing methods (particularly in services).

4) Structural evolution or morphogenesis (changing goals and changing environment).

To continue to exist in an environment that is evolving strongly or to seize an opportunity offered by this situation, the system decides to radically change its end purpose.

> *Examples of structural evolution: vertical integration, withdrawal of a significant part of business activity (e.g. keeping only commercialization activities and research and development (R&D), diversification outside current sectors and modifying the logic of client relationship (e.g. offering access to a commodity rather than ownership of a commodity). A number of strategic actions recommended by Porter [POR 85], the effects of which modify the structure of an entire sector, are typical of structural evolution.*

These four levels and the aforementioned typology (operational, tactical and strategic) correspond as follows:

– the operational level is that of regulation;

– the tactical level is that of functional adaptation and structural adaptation (in part);

– the strategic level is that of structural adaptation (in part) and structural evolution.

1.3.7. *Toward decision support for the three management levels*

From very early days, the domain recognized that the requirements of decision support, and more broadly information, differed 'a great deal depending on the decision level [GOR 71, SIM 60]. In the same way that it is difficult to differentiate between decisions and actions [SIM 97], the decision levels are closely interconnected. In fact, any strategic decision will be conveyed by a set of tactical decisions, each of which is, in turn, the subject of a number of operational decisions. A large number of pieces of research into DSS have, however, failed to specify which level(s) of decisions they were seeking to support. Meanwhile, the majority of tools available on the market have shown themselves to be principally focused on operational decisions.

Since 1980, Sprague, defining a general framework for DSS design, has pleaded that:

> DSS should provide decision making support for managers *at all levels* [our emphasis], assisting in integration between the levels whenever appropriate.

This book subscribes to this approach: it is an ambitious goal for the domain and, for the most part, has not yet been achieved. To try to achieve this objective, research into decision support should always specify the level(s) of decisions they concern.

1.3.8. *Standardizing decisions*

The organizations within which decisions are made determine in part, of course, not only the content of decisions, but they also influence the extent to which they are *structured*. At the extreme end of the continuum mentioned by Simon (between non-programmed and programmed decisions or unstructured or structured decisions), the organization may have produced decisions which are made via a totally standardized process. Structured decisions may, therefore, have been the subject of *standardization* (by internal or external standards).

For example: the decision of an airline's customer service to authorize or not authorize the modification of flight dates (a procedure inscribed in tariff-types); a buyer's decision to place an order (related to stock levels depending on the period, etc.) and; a commercial manager's decision to accept or not accept an order (checking the solvency of the client).

Some decisions may be structured (the decision maker in question can describe the structure of the problem the decision must solve as well as the process for solving it), although they have not yet been the subject of standardization within the organization.

For instance, choosing a new supplier, recruiting a new employee, etc.

By definition, unstructured decisions cannot be the subject of standardization.

Nowadays, highly standardized decision-making is often part of production software (in the broad sense) and, therefore, no longer appears as decision-making but rather as a simple procedure (which may sometimes make adjusting to an unexpected situation difficult).

1.3.9. *Taking into account the dynamic of organizations and their environment*

Over the past 30 years, enterprises, like all institutions, have witnessed big changes in the way they and their environment operate. In the field of decision support, many papers justify the growing interest in DSS by the need of enterprises to adjust to a constantly changing economic environment, characterized by the globalization of all exchanges (commodities and services, financial flows, human resources and information).

For some authors, these changes to organizations' environment have a strong impact on decision-making, particularly given that the numbers of undefined problems and unstructured decisions have multiplied. Mitroff and Linstone [MIT 93] therefore believe that business leaders must radically change their way of thinking to tackle these new situations. Following in their footsteps, Courtney [COU 01] suggests that research into decision support should "change paradigm" to take new dimensions into account during DSS design (organizational, personal, ethical, etc.).

In our opinion, these considerations do not go far enough. We believe it to be impossible to work in DSS design without focusing on the *sense* of decisions (their content). The latter is, in fact, a direct function of the dynamic of the organization within which the decision is made; this dynamic is itself closely connected to the dynamic of the environment.

Although, as previously mentioned, the importance of changes to the environment is broadly recognized in the domain, very few studies do more than merely take note of its existence. Our position is that to improve decision makers and organizations' understanding of current requirements, it is essential to conduct a detailed analysis into the nature of these evolutions and the type of impact they have on organization management. This analysis can only be conducted via *interdisciplinarity*, i.e. by borrowing the elements required from other domains, in this case for the most part from economics.

1.4. Changes to management within organizations

This section will describe the changes to management within organizations. Four dimensions will be the focus: connections with the environment, the stability of boundaries, innovation and requirements linked to IS.

1.4.1. *Connections with the environment*

In terms of the basic strategic choice of "to make or to buy", enterprises have successively adopted three types of response.

The dominant strategy during the *Glorious Thirty* (1947–1974) was to seek to be independent from the environment and opt for vertical integration (upstream and/or downstream). Connections with the environment were therefore reduced, stable and not very complex. The roles of different players (clients, suppliers, competitors, research partners, etc.) were well defined, stable and had little or no overlap. The logic of commercialization was totally focused on expanding the enterprise's part of the market (keeping clients seemed obvious). In this first phase, understanding the environment was relatively easy.

In the *second* transitional *period*, there was an intensification in external procurement [MOA 08]. Known as quasi-integration logic, enterprises contracted out part of their production on the basis of precise specifications. Even though they maintained expertise about and control over their subproducts, enterprises had to contend with a new type of player and partner (subcontractors).

Demand grew fast both in intensity (characteristic peaks and falls) and content (expectation of variety at the level of the offer). Consumers were no longer a global mass that could be lumped into the one dimension of buying power. New categories emerged besides the socio-professional categories. Market segmentation, therefore, became a key factor for enterprises: markets were broken down into increasingly smaller markets (which later became "niche markets"). Environment analysis mostly focused on consumer behavior and their evolution.

In the *third period,* which started in the 1980s and is currently ongoing, there has been a shift from a logic of integration (or quasi-integration) toward a logic of *outsourcing,* which is accompanied by a pronounced financialization of strategies (particularly for large groups). The control of its by-products is no longer provided by the company, which relies on co-contractors, on the basis of functional needs or problems to be solved, rather than on the basis of complete technical specifications. A central concern is determining the enterprise's core skills and thus the knowledge and skills the enterprise must continue to hold. A detailed understanding of changes to the environment across all levels (client requirements, competition, trends in scientific and technical research, etc.) becomes essential. This process of understanding requires large volumes of reliable and often qualitative information and involves the complex task of interpreting it, which must often be done in a group.

1.4.2. *Boundaries*

The nature of the enterprise's boundaries has changed a great deal over the three periods, whether they be boundaries separating the enterprise from its environment, boundaries separating the different markets and boundaries demarcating the activity sectors.

In the *first period,* boundaries were stable, airtight and easy to identify. This is true for the boundary separating the enterprise from its environment, even the closest environment. Similarly, sectors (as defined by the National Institutes of Statistics) were based on a stable triptych (one market, one product and one technology) [GUI 71] and constituted a division from the economic activities. Enterprises, with a few rare exceptions (very large enterprises), operated on a local, regional or national level.

In the *second period*, the market and sector boundaries remained relatively stable, but there was a clear shift toward the international (markets, competition, looking for subcontractors, etc.).

It is during the *third period* that there has been a radical change in the question of boundaries. The enterprise's boundaries shifted to embrace the system it had formed with all its partners and thereby defined the space in which the enterprise operated, made decisions, was organized and structured its IS [SHI 02].

The development of key enabling technologies (e.g. digital) has destabilized the aforementioned triptych (one market, one product and one technology) [SAL 07b]. Boundaries between the sectors, as determined in classifications, lose much of their relevance [COL 10] and become porous. Market boundaries are blurred and the markets are thus "questionable"[4] [BAU 82]. There is a shift from a logic of the product, production process or market to a logic of skills which induces greater movement in business activity. For the enterprise, this produces both opportunities (new markets, new requirements leading to the design of new products, new technologies, etc.) and threats (new competitors with the same products or with substitute products, fast and radical obsolescence of manufacturing processes, etc.).

In line with a picture of activities and markets that are in constant flux, an enterprise's competitors are a changing group. New incomers arrive from "foreign" sectors and from countries which had not hitherto operated in the nation in question. Competitors offering substitution products, rather than identical products, pose the biggest

---

4 When an enterprise can cross the boundaries of a market when the dominant technology is the same (e.g. IT toward telecommunications).

threat. Identifying current and potential competitors requires a mass of information and excellent analysis skills.

In this period, operating spaces became international for all players: clients, suppliers, subcontractors, workers, researchers, standards, etc. Players and flows (of information, funding, materials, products and workers) are moving, sometimes extremely fast, and are in operation over a global space. Once again, knowledge of the environment is decisive.

1.4.3. *Innovation*

Over the *first two periods*, innovation was mostly conducted internally. At the end of the second period, there was a shift from innovating the product and processes toward innovations concerning all sectors in the enterprise.

By the *third period*, there is no doubt that innovation became the primary factor for competition [MOA 08]. All sectors in the enterprise are obliged to innovate: product definitions, manufacturing processes, market segmentation, methods, the organization, the IS, etc. This approach focuses more on *creation* (new processes, new products, new markets, etc.) than on *conquest* (part of an existing market). A condition of this creation is the enterprise's ability to generate innovative representations (of its skills, markets, products, economic environment, etc.). In our opinion, one of the key roles of decision support (and more broadly IS) is to help managers to build these innovative representations.

1.4.4. *Requirements linked to information systems*

In the *first period*, as the enterprise's performance was based on factors (namely capital and work), information requirements principally concerned operational functioning.

The economic environment was considered stable in that the way it evolved was known and could therefore be predicted. Information on the environment was not specifically sought: it was considered to be obvious and/or available without effort.

Strategic decisions were made and applied over a long period. Many concerns were concentrated on decisions at the intermediary (tactical) and lower (operational) levels and focused on production organization. Problems often recurred and were mostly well defined. Decision-making was relatively easy and a high number of decisions could be optimized.

In the *second period*, the existence of production partners (subcontractors) complicated production management. In addition, more active competition gave a new importance to managing production projects (checking deadlines, costs, etc.).

The problems that needed to be solved remained relatively standardized. Logics of optimization were still possible for some decisions at the higher (choice of where to locate an establishment) or intermediary (defining the range, setting prices, scheduling production, etc.) levels. A part of operational decisions was spontaneously included in the procedures automatization software.

With the exception of information about consumer behavior, knowledge about the environment was not the focus of enterprises' concerns.

In the *third period,* the situation became much more complex and consequently there was a need for information and interpretation support. The rapid metamorphosis of the economic environment, the blurred and moving nature of all boundaries, the versatility of the positions of players and the constant search for innovation multiplied the number of previously unseen and unstructured problems at all levels of the enterprise's management. Solving these problems required creating new knowledge. This required information to be provided about the environment, the internal operations of the enterprise as well as about knowledge that had already been created (knowledge base, return on experience, etc.). In this context, the figures of the cognitive worker [COL 08] and the knowledge worker [ROS 08] became essential.

The constant need for internal and external coordination results in the need for specific technologies. In the event of a crisis, the latter must be capable of enabling players to solve complex problems together [HAN 12, BÉN 08], even if they have never cooperated together in the past.

Defining ranges, segmenting clients and setting prices have become very complex due to newcomers (potentially) entering the market and consumer movement, which is sometimes extreme. The IS used for decision support must provide both the necessary information (collected from internal and/or external sources) and interpretation support (data mining, simulation models, heuristics, etc.).

With regard to consumers, winning client loyalty is of primary importance. There are two reasons for this: first, the cost of keeping clients is much lower than the cost of expanding the client base and, second, only a long-term relationship can enable the enterprise to conduct an in-depth analysis into the needs and aspirations of consumers so as to constantly offer them new services based (or not based) on new products. In-depth knowledge about behavior (which tends to consider each client individually) becomes an essential factor for competition. IS, and specifically their digital part, must therefore store and process very detailed and historic information about clients and prospects (particularly using data warehouses).

In the third period, the industrial sector of business intelligence emerged (in the early 1980s) and then, logically in terms of the aforementioned requirements, experienced rapid and continued development. More modestly, technology intelligence moved away from R&D services alone and reinvented itself as strategic intelligence and then competitive intelligence. Its principal role was, therefore, to support the construction of innovative representations of the enterprise's environment and the inscription of the latter in the former.

Recent developments in the economic situation have given rise to new requirements, which can be categorized into two types. First, the financialization of strategies, which makes raising share value the mission of the enterprise and tends to some degree to uniformalize management and decision-making methods and, consequently, requirements for decision support. We believe that the great interest in Big Data originates from this trend (see Chapter 3). The second type of new requirements is concerned with group decision-making. This involves a large number of stakeholders, knowledge sharing about the enterprise's environment and taking ethical questions into account during decision-making.

1.4.5. *Changes to public institutions: territorial authorities*

Territorial authorities have experienced changes similar to those mentioned above. This section will describe some of the impacts of these changes.

1.4.5.1. *From government to governance*

In territorial authorities, there has been a shift from a logic of local or regional government – involving only elected representatives and services, on the one hand, and the State, on the other hand – toward a logic of governance, involving a diverse array of players (the European Union (EU), devolved State services, public institutions, enterprises, advice services, representatives of civil society, intermediary bodies, etc.).

1.4.5.2. *Expansion of the environment*

Territorial authorities, and especially the regions, have experienced a considerable expansion of their environment. When looking for foreign direct investment (FDI), they find themselves in competition not only with other regions in the country, but also with regions from other countries, which are often outside Europe. The same is true with regard to attracting qualified workers or looking for partners. In addition, the systematized practice of benchmarking results in authorities comparing themselves or being compared to authorities that are sometimes very distant (in all senses of the word).

1.4.5.3. *From territories with defined borders to the revelation of territories*

Alongside the need for governance and the expansion of the environment, defining the borders (of territories) has become more complex. For many years, invariant and hierarchized administrative borders (town, councils and counties) or borders produced by the National Institutes of Statistics (living zones and employment zones) have been the only borders used to identify territories. Nowadays, new types of non-hierarchized and evolving administrative entities are appearing: provinces (which can straddle several counties or even regions), communities of towns or urban areas, etc.

However, more crucially, there has been a change in paradigm: nowadays a territory (e.g. where a project is to be launched) can no longer be considered to be preexisting in the state; on the contrary, it is the end result of the players' actions throughout a project. The territory is, therefore, no longer identified before the project begins; it is revealed during the project.

1.4.5.4. *Requirements related to information and decision support*

The complexity produced by the aforementioned changes, the expansion of authorities' missions and simultaneously the reduction of their financial resources make reflecting on the definition of the management system an unavoidable task. The system of objectives must be explained, action variables determined, sensors defined, etc. A specific and very significant case is that of indicators. Evaluation needs can respond to regulatory requirements (e.g. issued from the State or the EU) relating to the use of received funds. The evaluation format is, therefore, set by the authority and the use of indicators is specifically required. Evaluation needs do, however, go well beyond this framework and refer to global issues of territorial development and to governance requirements (return toward the internal and external players in the authority, toward "normal" citizens, etc.).

New needs relating to information and decision support also arise from governance, which presupposes that the territorial authority cooperates with multiple players. The authority must be capable of identifying players, understanding their needs, defining projects in cooperation with them, managing their multi-party implementation, conducting a shared evaluation, etc. This implies, on the one hand, a territorial IS that is really capable of producing a formalized representation of all or part of the resources in the territory and, on the other hand, a set of collaborative and decision support tools.

Recognizing territorial authorities' need for specific information about the environment has resulted in the notion of territorial intelligence, which developed out of competitive intelligence [ADI 03]. A specific market offer rapidly succeeded this arrival: intelligence tools, information sources, advice, etc. This relatively recent activity has not yet (for the most part) been assessed, but territorial intelligence is without doubt one response to the needs resulting from changes to how territorial authorities function.

Conclusion: key points for DSS design

Choice of the general approach

The first point is the choice of the general DSS design approach. This approach can either be *normative* decision theory or the theory of decision *engineering*. Normative theory considers decision-making to be looking for the optimum: all useful information is known and available. The theory of decision engineering, in line with "historic" definitions of DSS, concentrates on weakly structured or unstructured decisions. The focus is thus on the *process* of decision-making throughout all its phases. The type of DSS and engineering requirements for its design differ a great deal depending on which of these two approaches is adopted. The first approach is actually more of an automatization of decision-making rather than decision support.

Main phase addressed by the DSS

A second positioning element concerns the phase (or phases) of the decision-making process that is considered central for the development of the DSS and/or that we are primarily seeking to support. In previously unseen and badly or undefined decision-making situations, the problem definition phase takes center stage. Conversely, in repetitive situations corresponding to structured and even standardized decision-making, the final phase – choice – will be the focus.

Decisions that define the management system or action decisions

A distinction must also be made between decisions related to the partial or global *definition of the management system* (defining the system of objectives, decision-making latitudes, indicators, etc.) and *action decisions* (action variables). In the majority of cases, decision support needs, decision support tools and the consequences of decisions are not the same for the two types of decisions.

Management level

It is also useful to determine the *management level* of the decisions we want to support. Decisions have very different goals and impacts depending on their level (operational, tactical or strategic). Similarly, decision support needs are mostly specific to each level. An understanding of the distinctive traits of each of the three levels must be included in any engineering requirements for DSS. The level(s) of decisions a DSS seeks to support should be clearly stated.

Innovation in decision-making

Finally, the relationship the DSS we are designing has with *innovation in decision-making* must be established. The organization within which the decisions are made is itself immersed in an environment with which it interacts. Over the past 20 years, this environment has experienced structural changes which have had a large impact on organization management. The extreme densification of connections with the environment, the constant questioning of all boundaries, the multiplication of players and the instability of their respective positions create new problems, which call for new and innovative decision-making. Supporting innovation in decision-making implies going beyond what already exists in decision-making to help decision makers build *new representations*.

Decision Support Systems

Introduction: DSS, tools for decision makers and for the organization

Decision support systems (DSS) are a component of the information system (IS) and, more specifically, of its information technology (IT) part, i.e. the IT or digital systems. They are based on representations of the organization and its environment, which are required for management, and which the IS and the IT system have formalized.

A distinction must be made between DSS and – what we are calling here conventional – IT systems, which concentrate on the automatization of production systems, i.e. tasks enabling the mission to be concretely realized (see section 1.3.1). DSS and conventional IT systems have different goals, design methods, relationships with the users and, for the most part, technical tools.

In the domain of research, the English-speaking world uses one term: DSS[1]. The emergence and then the rapid development of the market of IT decision-making tools produced new names. Among the latter, the term *business intelligence* (BI), invented at the end of the

---

1 In French, decision support systems have produced a number of different names: information decision support systems as well as interactive decision support and even IT decision support systems (all of which have the same acronym in French, "SIAD").

1980s by Howard Dresner from the Gartner Group [NYL 99], became widely used.

In this book, we will use the term DSS which belongs to the academic domain (unlike BI, which falls into the category of marketing language).

Section 2.1 will discuss the main definitions of what Gorry and Scott Morton [GOR 71] called *management decision systems* (MDS), which later became DSS. The standard components of a DSS will be briefly described and a number of typologies of decision support tools will then be set out. A brief history of research in the domain will then be described, which identifies four periods. The sector of BI will then be introduced and its main technical tools will be presented. The particular type of DSS that constitute Big Data will be specifically discussed. This section will conclude by describing the most common criticisms leveled against DSS, which principally concern their inability to respond to the decision makers' and the organization's needs.

Section 2.2 will discuss DSS engineering, which relates to design methods. Seligmann *et al.*'s [SEL 89] model, which describes a method comprising four components, will be used as a framework to present the elements of DSS design. The remainder of the section will concentrate on the requirements engineering phase, which is essential for matching the DSS to the needs of the decision makers and the organization, and evaluating its impact on all stakeholders, which is a critical point for us. Out of a number of different approaches, we will study in particular goal-driven requirements engineering. A number of examples of methods will then be presented.

2.1. DSS: definitions and typologies

2.1.1. *Definitions*

In a pioneering article published in 1971, Gorry and Scott Morton [GOR 71] suggested making a distinction between management information systems (MIS) and what they called MDS.

Very complete and still relevant today, Gorry and Scott Morton's text clearly lays out the main problems of the domain and demonstrates that MIS are broadly dedicated to the automatization of operational tasks. In terms of decision-making, MIS focus on structured decisions, which mostly correspond to the decision level with the smallest range: the operational level, as defined in Chapter 1, or operational control, according to Anthony's [ANT 65] typology. Stating that the needs for weakly structured or unstructured decisions and/or higher level decisions (tactical and strategic) are not met by MIS, they present a general framework to develop digital IS capable of helping these types of decisions – MDS – which are presented as follows:

> It is (the) semi-structured [decision] area where the interactive terminal systems have their greatest potential. [these] Decisions (…) are largely unstructured and we have chosen to term information systems that support these Management Decision Systems (MDS).

From the very start, DSS are therefore set against, on the one hand, conventional IT systems (automatization of procedures) and, on the other hand, logics aiming to optimize decisions (normative approach), which, by definition, can only be applied to structured decisions. It should be noted that at the same time, the normative approach to decision-making moved into operational research, which sought to identify the optimal choices in decision-making.

Gorry and Scott Morton's "historic" definition has never really been challenged, although it has been refined and/or expanded. A few years later, Keen and Scott Morton [KEE 78] confirmed that:

> DSS are computer-based support for management decision makers who are dealing with semi-structured problems.

From a literature review and implementations, Sprague [SPR 80] observed that the DSS has four characteristics, the first of which describes the types of decisions dealt with by DSS:

They tend to be aimed at the less well-structured, underspecified problems that upper level managers typically face.

Sprague and Carlson [SPR 82] refine and add to the previous definitions by characterizing DSS as:

(…) *interactive* computer-based systems that *help* decision makers utilize *data* and *models* to solve *unstructured* problems.

The terms in italics (the author's emphasis) show the specificities of decision support. The function of a DSS is, therefore, to *help* the decision maker and not to replace him or her. Decision support is therefore, once again, set against optimization.

Further research has either refined or considerably expanded the definition of DSS. In the case of the former, definitions detail the necessary qualities (interactive, flexible and adaptable) [TUR 95] or the components of the system ("data base management systems with analytical and operational research models, graphic display, tabular reporting capabilities") ([FIS 96] quoted by [BOE 10]). In the case of the latter, definitions only reference the IT system and decision-making. Finlay [FIN 94] simply wrote:

DSS is a computer-based system that aids the process of decision making.

The emergence and then the rapid development of the market of BI produced new definitions and names. Among the latter, the term *business intelligence system*, invented in the late 1980s by Howard Dresner from the Gartner Group [NYL 99], became widely used from the late 1990s [POW 07]. Power [POW 09] even quotes a glossary compiled by the IBM [IBM 09], which defines DSS as:

(…) one of a number of older synonyms for application and data used to support decision-making and business management processes, now broadly called business intelligence systems.

It currently seems that the term *BI* belongs to the commercial domain, whereas the academic domain continues to use the term "decision support system" (DSS).

Without contradicting Sprague and Carlson's definition, many more recent definitions have deliberately left the field very open. This is true for the definition of DSS proposed by Shim *et al.* [SHI 02]:

> Decision support systems (DSS) are computer technology solutions that can be used to support complex decision making and problem solving

and in Arnott's [ARN 08b] definition presenting the domain:

> Decision support systems (DSS) is the area of the information systems (IS) discipline that is focused on supporting and improving managerial decision-making.

2.1.2. *Standard components of a decision support system*

Sprague [SPR 80] describes the technical components of a DSS as:

> (...) database management software (DBMS), model base management software (MBMS), and the software for managing the interface between the user and the system, which might be called the dialogue generation and management software (DGMS).

A DSS is, therefore, composed of several modules which, respectively, manage:

– data (potentially all types);

– models (statistical, financial, accounting, optimization, etc.);

– the dialogue between the user and the DSS (human–machine interface (HMI)).

This list of three (very global) components has since been widely used.

The notion of data can be understood in a very broad sense to include documents (text and non-text) and, more generally, codified knowledge[2]. It should be noted that in some lists of the standard components comprising DSS, this knowledge is the subject of a fourth specific category.

It should be noted that if we consider the DSS from an organizational perspective, we should add its essential "component": the user(s).

An example of the architecture is provided in Figure 2.1.

2.1.3. *Typologies of decision support systems*

DSS have resulted in researchers and industrial players producing a number of classifications. Two such typologies are presented below.

2.1.3.1. *Typology based on realized operations*

Alter [ALT 80] proposed one of the first typologies of DSS. He classified DSS according to the main operations they realize on an axis spanning from the most data-driven DSS to the most model-driven DSS. He identified seven categories (numbered here from 1 to 7) and which Power [POW 01] suggested grouping into three categories (listed here from A to C):

A) Data-driven DSS:

1) file drawer systems;

2) data analysis systems, which aid data handling by generic- or task-specific operators and tools;

3) analysis IS, which enable access to decision-driven databases and use a limited number of data processing models.

---

2 At this point, we are using the term "knowledge" as it is commonly used in this context, but later we will make a distinction between data, information and knowledge, and will provide precise definitions of these three concepts (Chapter 3, section 3.2.4.3.).

B) Model-driven DSS:

4) accounting and financial models that calculate the impacts of the proposed decisions (using data from analytical accounting);

5) representational models which evaluate the consequences of the actions intended to support simulation models;

6) optimization models that generate an optimal choice.

C) Knowledge-driven DSS:

7) suggestion models that carry out logical processing and suggest a decision (in the case of well-structured decisions).

Power [POW 04] expanded this framework by adding two new categories, both of which are also based on the main component of the DSS: document-driven DSS and communications-driven DSS. He also suggested three other secondary dimensions, which concern the users (internal and/or external to the organization), the function of the DSS and the implementation technology. Table 2.1 summarizes this classification.

2.1.3.2. A mixed typology

Many other typologies exist, such as Arnott's [ARN 08b], which combines a number of dimensions (number of decision makers, use/purpose and technology) to finally identify seven types of DSS:

– *personal DSS*: usually small-scale systems that are normally developed for one manager, or a small number of independent managers, for one decision task;

– *group support systems*: the use of a combination of communication and DSS technologies to facilitate the effective working of groups;

– *negotiation support systems*: DSS where the primary focus of the group work is negotiation between opposing parties;

– *intelligent DSS*: the application of artificial intelligence techniques to DSS;

– *knowledge management-based DSS*: systems that support decision-making by aiding knowledge storage, retrieval, transfer and application by supporting individual and organizational memory and inter-group knowledge access;

– *executive information systems/business intelligence*: data-oriented and model-oriented DSS that provide reporting about the nature of an organization to management;

– *data warehousing*: systems that provide the large-scale data infrastructure for decision support.

Dominant DSS component	Target users *Internal => External*	Purpose *General => Specific*	Deployment/enabling technology
Communications Communications-driven DSS	Internal teams, now expanding to external partners	Conduct a meeting or help users collaborate	Web or client/server
Database Data-driven DSS	Managers, staff, now suppliers	Query a data warehouse	Main frame, Client/server, web
Document base Document-driven DSS	Internal users, but the user group is expanding	Search webpages or find documents	Web or client/server
Knowledge base Knowledge-driven DSS	Internal users, now customers	Management advice or choose products	Client/server, web, stand-alone PC
Models Model-driven DSS	Managers and staff, now customers	Crew scheduling or decision analysis	Stand-alone PC or client/server or web

Table 2.1. *An expanded DSS framework [POW 01]*

In our opinion, the multiplication of the classification dimensions expresses first and foremost the limits of the exercise of DSS classification. With the exception, perhaps, of data warehouses (and Big Data), DSS are not based on proprietary technologies and any classification based on technical aspects is likely to explain very little as many DSS combine several technologies. Typologies based on needs and use (personal, group, negotiation, etc.) take the greatest account of differences existing in the development process of a DSS.

2.1.3.3. The specific case of competitive intelligence

Competitive intelligence is a domain that focuses on aiding decision-making by providing information about the organization's *environment*. Competitive intelligence watches the environment thus favoring an understanding of it and the emergence of innovative views about it. Strangely, competitive intelligence has never really merged with the domain of DSS and the tools it proposes remain relatively disconnected from DSS tools. Nevertheless, the future of competitive intelligence lies in its ability to integrate decision support methods and tools [SAL 06].

2.1.4. A brief history of research in the domain

Over the course of its history, the domain of DSS has passed through three main periods, and a fourth is, probably, about to begin.

2.1.4.1. Period 1: very open research

The first period (from the early 1970s to the mid-1980s) was very open and laid down the conceptual foundations of the domain [POW 07]. Research was based explicitly on work produced in other disciplines about decision-making ([SIM 60, CYE 63], etc.) and management ([ANT 65, ANS 88], etc.) and adopted an engineering approach. In Simon's intelligence, design, choice (IDC) process, all phases were considered, with a clear focus on phase 1 (intelligence).

2.1.4.2. Period 2: the domination of techniques

The second period (from the 1980s to the early 2000s) focused on techniques. Research concentrated on tools and the industrial sector (see below) emerged and rapidly developed. In 1992, Hofstede remarked:

There is a general agreement among DSS researchers that the D in DSS has not received proper attention.

Within the decision process, most attention was paid to the *design* and *choice* phases. Many tools, therefore, included techniques that were more of an automatization (or optimization) of decision-making rather than decision-making support. Returning to the topic of problem formulation in the decision-making process, Shim *et al.* [SHI 02] commented:

> The technical perspective has dominated DSS problem formulation in the past (...).

The end of this period was marked by debates about the specificities of DSS [PEA 95], and reflections about the effectiveness of DSS and more broadly ITs in improving decision-making. Davenport [DAV 99] warns us against what he calls the "technological obsession" remarking that:

> Studies on managers show that the information currently at their disposal is barely an improvement on what they had before.

2.1.4.3. *Period 3: diversification and the return of decision-making*

The third period, which started in the late 1990s and is currently ongoing (or is about to end, see below), saw a diversification of the topics discussed.

Technological aspects mostly concerned Web-based DSS development [BHA 07, NEB 12], processing knowledge [AZA 12, ZHU 13], open data and Big Data [CHE 12], in cloud DSS development [DEM 13] and mobile applications [ELH 11].

However, although technologies have occupied a considerable section of research, new or renewed questions have been asked. Shim *et al.* [SHI 02] quoted [KEE 87] to remind researchers that:

> The DSS technology itself is not important – it is the support we intend to provide which is the key element.

Group decision-making has become a topic in its own right; based on both general (groupware) and specific tools, it faces the same problems of knowledge management [ARD 13].

In Simon's decision process, the focus is set on the upstream part of the *intelligence* phase, i.e. being aware of the need to make a decision and defining the problem. The risks associated with this phase have been recognized [MIT 97]. In DSS development, emphasis is placed on needs analysis whose complexity and issues are better perceived. A number of authors stress the need to take into account not only a broad set of stakeholders, but also the existence of different and even contrasting perspectives or points of view [MIT 93]. This will be dealt with in Chapter 3.

Finally, this third period saw the modest emergence of *ethical* concerns. Some authors have recognized the designer's responsibility for the decisions made with the help of the developed DSS [MER 03, CHA 05, MAT 07a]. We will return to the topic of ethics in DSS design in Chapter 4.

2.1.4.4. *The rapid growth of Big Data: the beginning of a fourth period?*

The rapid development of research and markets related to Big Data may, by their specificities, bring about the start of a fourth period. This phase would be characterized by major upheavals to decision-making methods and processes, particularly with regard to public decision-making (we will return to this topic in Chapter 3). Given the importance of this technology, we will deal with this topic in detail in section 2.1.6.

2.1.5. *Business intelligence*

2.1.5.1. *Some details about the business intelligence sector*

The BI market has experienced continuous growth since its inception in the 1990s. Unlike ITs market, it suffered very little during the 2001 crisis (when the Internet bubble burst) and the years that followed, with an annual growth of over 10%. Growth has not really slowed since 2008 [GAR 12] particularly due to demand from the public sector, the financial sector and large-scale distribution.

Professionals expect to see significant growth over the coming years due to Big Data, increased numbers of users in organizations, ease of use and personalized applications (a non-expert has the option to really dialog with the DSS, mobile applications, etc.). Figures about the Big Data market will not be provided as they vary a great deal and appear to have been relatively overestimated.

2.1.5.2. *Some business intelligence tools*

The first specific tools for decision support appeared in the 1980s with executive information systems (EIS).

The next decade witnessed the revolution of online analytical processing (OLAP), which enables multi-dimensional analysis (e.g. revenue seen on geographic, time, product and client axes) to be conducted from databases or data warehouses (the latter emerged in the same period). The multi-dimensional view is conceptualized through a hypercube (hyper because it can have more than three dimensions).

Data warehouses require specific tools such as extract-transform-load (ETL), which enables the warehouse to be automatically loaded from the source databases. Specialized tools enable queries to be built (query tools) and reports, dashboards, analyses, etc., to be produced (reporting tools).

Datamarts gather a set of relatively reduced data (compared with data warehouses) about one department in the enterprise (financial, HR management, marketing, commercial, etc.). The data can come from databases from the conventional IT system and external sources, but what we most often call a "datamart" is a subset of a data warehouse.

Large volumes of data are processed using data mining, text mining and web mining tools. The algorithms enabling processing come from statistics and artificial intelligence.

Figure 2.1 shows an example of the architecture of a data-driven DSS.

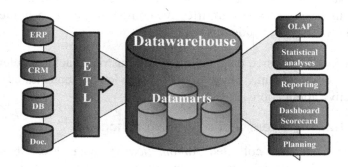

Figure 2.1. *Simplified diagram of a data warehouse*

For the past dozen years, BI tools have been adapted to the web (user interfaces, data sources, etc.) and, more recently, to mobile applications.

It should be noted that spreadsheets (e.g. Excel) are largely used in BI as a tool for presenting results (dashboards, scorecards, etc.) and developing complete applications as well as a support for prototyping.

2.1.6. *A specific type of decision support tool: Big Data*

In recent years, Big Data has appeared, particularly in the decision support (or its automatization) sector, accompanied by massive media campaigns in the USA and then in Europe, which boast their considerable capacities to analyze the real and predict its evolution.

Given the importance of these techniques, their relative novelty and specificities, we will now detail the principal characteristics of Big Data and a number of their uses for decision support.

2.1.6.1. *Characteristics*

Big Data differs from traditional databases and even data warehouses due to a set of characteristic and interrelated traits.

2.1.6.1.1. The diversity of sources

Sources can be human beings: data are, therefore, collected about their state (health, location, etc.), their behavior and even their emotions (see the domain of affective computing) or, to a limited but growing extent, their thoughts.

Sources of massive data can also be industrial machines, elements of the environment, other sets of previously constituted data, interactive applications, etc.

2.1.6.1.2. The diversity of collection methods

Data can be collected *automatically*: data are, therefore, automatically sent by sensors (components of ubiquitous or ambient computing, or connected devices: geolocalization sensors in a mobile device, physical state sensors in a machine, data sensors related to a person's health, such as their heart rate, etc.) and computer devices (purchases by credit card). It can be automatically recovered from other internal ("classic" enterprise databases) or external (e.g. climatic and demographic data) sources.

A trend has been observed: automatic data collection is expanding both in terms of the volumes of data being captured (particularly via connected devices) and the diversity of the data (see the recent developments in neuromarketing which are based on sensors capturing eye movement, electrical activity in the brain, etc.).

Collection can also be generated by the uses people make of the Internet: surfing online, exchanges on social networks, purchases made, queries entered on a search engine, participation on discussion forums, phone numbers called, blogs, etc.

2.1.6.1.3. The volume of data and its rapid growth

The numerous press articles about Big Data, manufacturers' advertising in the sector as well as a number of research papers stress the substantial volumes of this data (as a gauge of performance). The measurement units currently used are the terabyte (10^{12} bytes) and the petabyte (10^{15}), but the future promises the exabyte (10^{18}), the zettabyte (10^{21}) and even the yottabyte (10^{24}).

The speed at which these volumes are growing is awe-inspiring, with rates of data produced expected to double every 18 or 24 months, particularly due to the spread of connected devices.

Big Data is historicized data (like in data warehouses) which, therefore, accumulates over time. Its growth is partly due to a very short collection period, which is sometimes less than 1 s.

2.1.6.1.4. The diversity of the types of data and the high number of dimensions

The types of data processed are heterogeneous. Data can, therefore, be structured or unstructured and of different types: texts, numerical values, images, sounds, etc. The granularity of the data is generally quite fine and the tendency is to make it increasingly finer. A very high number of dimensions are considered.

2.1.6.1.5. Associated types of processing

The types of processing (comparable with those used in data mining) can be grouped into two categories which correspond to two successive phases: data analysis and model development.

The raw data require initial processing to prepare it. Initial processing involves storing only the most relevant data with regard to the objectives of the organization behind the device, as well as correcting the identifiable errors it contains, filling in missing data, etc. The latter is comparable to processing for data warehouses via ETL.

Pre-prepared data are then processed using statistical calculations (looking for correlations), decision trees, semantic analysis and artificial intelligence techniques.

This involves identifying structures, associations and, more generally, patterns in the data. It should be noted that the effectiveness of the processing relies, partly, on the presence and the quality of the metadata describing the data collected.

According to players in the sector, the major issue for Big Data is *predictive* processing. Predictive models are developed on the basis of the analyses conducted, which are, for the moment, based on relatively classic techniques, but which sometimes use a very high number of variables. These models are known as Big Data *algorithms*. It is worth noting that the algorithms of the biggest players in the domain, primarily Google, are not publicly available, and as such the way in which the announced results are obtained is unknown and thus cannot be questioned. Self-learning capacities (from artificial intelligence) are included in some predictive analysis algorithms so as to improve the effectiveness of the models. One of the objectives stated was to reach, beyond mere prediction, *prescriptive* models (that indicate which decisions must be made).

These models are incorporated into decision support applications whose human–machine interface broadly uses displays (graphs, etc.) to show the results and help their handling.

Given the very large volumes that need to be processed, a major issue for all these algorithms is their processing speed, which is for the moment the real specificity of massive data processing algorithms. Descriptive statistical analysis, predictive models or heterogeneous and unstructured data processing, etc., have in fact (in some cases) existed for a very long time and are used in countless applications outside the domain of Big Data.

From a strictly technical point of view, Big Data does not for the moment constitute a disruptive innovation. Given that very large volumes need to be processed, technical evolutions have accompanied the development of Big Data and its uses. Specific data models (replacing relational models), storage methods (often distributed) and, as previously mentioned, algorithms specialized in processing large volumes in short periods, sometimes in quasi-real time, have therefore emerged. In addition, Big Data uses non-specific techniques, such as cloud computing, massively parallel architectures, systems of sensors, networks, etc.

However, although there has been no disruptive innovation from the technical perspective, the very broad and multi-faceted uses that promoters of Big Data have fervently promised will undoubtedly lead to a significant transformation of society. By way of comparison, it is the massive number of Internet users and the multiplicity of uses that have led to an effect of innovation, rather than the technologies on which it is built, which existed well before its development.

2.1.6.1.6. Some current uses

Only uses related to decision support will be discussed, and as such applications of Big Data in the context of scientific research will not be described.

Decision support by Big Data can provide the type of support offered by data warehouses and the associated IT system, i.e. multi-dimensional analysis, but beyond this, it (as we have said) specifically aims to predict (human behavior, machine breakdowns, etc.). As such, it should be noted that the use of Big Data tends to position itself as an *alternative to human decision-making* (by prescribing the decision or automatic decision-making) rather than as a *support* to decision-making.

Some examples of uses are given below.

2.1.6.1.7. Decision support in private organizations

In marketing, the objective is to distribute (progressively) microsegments of the market to target groups of consumers and adapt the offer to their past or future behavior (predicted by massive data processing). This microsegmentation can include a local dimension (e.g. catchment area by sales point) and may eventually enable some decisions at this level to be automated (e.g. automatically modifying prices, etc.)[3]. The extreme degree of microsegmentation is the so-called "personalized" offer, which will be discussed later in this section.

Predicting behavior is also used in recruitment. First, the characteristics of the least/most efficient workers regarding the

---

3 technologies.lesechos.fr/business-intelligence/big-data-c-est-le-chef-de-rayon-qu-il-faut-former_a-41-506.html.

enterprise's criteria are analyzed (by processing the set of digital data about them). Then using these profiles, the candidates are compared. Likewise, an enterprise which has a high level of staff turnover can analyze the set of data available about workers who have left/stayed to understand the reasons why they left their jobs.

Results sometimes lack value. A press article[4] reported:

> Gate Gourmet, an enterprise providing catering services for airlines with around 1,000 employees at Chicago airport, was able to discover why its staff turnover rate reached 50%. By correlating demographic and geographic (traffic and public transport) data, the performance of the employee, their rate of pay and where they lived, the enterprise understood that there was a link between the resignation of its employees and geographic distance but also low pay.

In view of the fact that Big Data was required to reach this result, it is perfectly reasonable to question the common sense of the decision makers in this enterprise and the level of social dialogue that exists within it.

Wichita State University in the United States has tried out an application for the selection of its future students using all the digital data available about them (curriculum vitae (CVs), academic transcripts, as well as, of course, the traces left by their use of the Internet and social networks[5]).

Big Data is also used for the preventive maintenance of mechanical parts. Following the analysis of breakdown data, predictive models put together a schedule of when parts should be changed, calculated depending on the type of machine, its environment and its use.

---

4 www.journaldunet.com/management/expert/59003/big-data-en-recrutement–quelques-etudes-de-cas.shtml.
5 "Students: personal data from the web to replace the entrance exam", www.lalibre.be, 5 November 2014.

2.1.6.1.8. Influence on individual decisions

Analyzing a person's purchasing behavior and their inscription in a previously defined profile type (a set of characteristics common to a group) enables purchase suggestions to be made and targeted advertising to be displayed on the webpages of the individual consults. The most cited example is that of Amazon's "recommendations" system, which is reputed to have generated tens of millions of dollars of extra revenue.

It should be noted that by using this type of site, the user simultaneously provides information (which is poured into Big Data) and is the target of the results produced by this same Big Data.

The influence that can be exercised on consumer behavior is not new (no more than advertising) and was theorized in the 1920s by Edward Bernays, the father of the first opinion manipulation techniques. What Big Data brings to the table is a very detailed description of behaviors (due to the granularity of the data) as well as the ability to adapt very quickly to any identified modifications and even predict (probabilistically) the online user's next action.

2.1.6.1.9. Public decision support

The most celebrated example by sycophants of Big Data is undoubtedly the following: in 2009, Google allegedly obtained results about the spread of the H1N1 virus, not from data produced by health professionals (data which take 2 weeks to reach the authorities) but by researching (from a set of keywords) the queries entered into search engines, press articles, messages, blog posts, etc., and then processing them. The system (Google Flu Trends) could thus, supposedly, detect the zones at risk very quickly and in so doing position itself as a decision support tool for public health. As will be seen in Chapter 3, processing algorithms (like that of Google Flu Trends) produce errors that can be substantial. In the same chapter, a number of examples will be presented to illustrate the risks associated with certain uses of these large volumes of digital data in the context of decision support.

2.1.7. *Criticisms leveled at business intelligence*

DSS are the subject of recurrent criticisms. One of the major complaints leveled against them is their disconnection from the enterprise's strategy and, more broadly, their relative inability to support decisions with high added value (tactical or strategic), i.e. weakly structured or unstructured decisions [ARN 08a, SAL 09, BIT 11].

Furthermore, and according to a number of studies (analyses from the Gartner Group, BI Survey of the BARC, etc.), about 70% of BI projects fail, mostly because they do not meet users' needs. The reasons given for this failure primarily concern the definition of the system's objectives and the needs of its users, i.e. requirements engineering and, second, the way projects are managed.

The next section is dedicated to DSS engineering and focuses specifically on requirements engineering.

2.2. DSS engineering

Engineering is the discipline of "how to do". It relates to all the activities that enable a system (in the broad sense) to be produced, from the first idea to the concrete implementation of the system and its evolution (and even its replacement). The notions of precision, rationality and the application of scientific principles integrated into engineering methods are associated with it.

IT systems aiming to automate production systems, i.e. tasks enabling the mission to be concretely realized (see section 1.3.1), which we called conventional IT systems, have benefitted, practically since their inception, from reflections about the way in which they are designed (the notion of *software engineering* dates back to 1968). The latter resulted in methods and tools with a general and even universal aim and a set of standards shared by all professionals.

Conversely, in the domain of DSS, very few global methods have been proposed. A diverse array of approaches were designed by researchers [GAC 05, MAR 01], but no one particular approach seems to dominate nor have they been adopted by players in the BI sector. Methods have certainly emerged in the sector, but the majority of them remain related to tools (data warehouses, ETL, cubes and query tools) and more rarely to certain types of DSS (group, negotiation and knowledge-based) or application domains (medical, legal and risk management).

All of these methods remain very focused on the downstream design phases [FAY 96]. After years of being neglected, requirements analysis has in recent years become the subject of research projects (see section 2.2.3). Yet, as will be seen, design methods for conventional IT systems are difficult to apply to all design phases due to the specificities of DSS (section 2.2.3.1). Some of their components can, however, be used.

2.2.1. *The components of a design method for IT systems or DSS*

Seligmann *et al.* [SEL 89] put together a framework (or rather a meta-framework) that describes a design method for IT systems. This framework describes a method constituted of four components called "ways of":

– the way of thinking (the paradigm and the point of view);

– the way of modeling (the models to build);

– the way of organizing (the approach to follow);

– the way of supporting (support tools).

We will provide details about each of these components, describing them by the elements of the DSS design.

2.2.1.1. *Way of thinking (overall perspective and paradigm)*

The *way of thinking* concerns *paradigms* and, more broadly, the theory used to build the method. The theory determines the type of representation of the real that will be at work in the method, i.e. at the most general level, the epistemological perspective in which it is positioned and at a more specific level, the broad classifications of entities retained for future modeling. The *way of thinking* must also expose the points of view adopted about these entities.

The first (and for a long time the only) global DSS design method was Sprague and Carlson's representations, operations, memory, control (ROMC) method (from 1982). In their work, the authors clearly defined DSS (see section 2.1.1, their definition remains canonical) and their components. They explicitly aligned themselves with Simon's work by reproducing the phase of the IDC process in the steps of their method.

Current methods, with a few rare exceptions (see the business intelligence model (BIM) requirements engineering method later), do not present the theory on which they are based, let alone their epistemological perspective. They consider as *given* elements which, in our opinion, are not and should be the result of transparent choices: list of project stakeholders, the enterprise's mission, global sense of the evaluation by the indicators, the share of quantitative data in the data, etc. We will return to this topic in Chapter 4.

2.2.1.2. Way of modeling (modeling)

The *way of modeling* deals with the *models* to produce and the way in which they are developed and formalized. Modeling produces a formalized representation of the entities (and more broadly the knowledge) used in the method.

Modeling can be realized according to the procedures broadly shared by a community (e.g. object-driven modeling) or *ad hoc* procedures with a high degree of formalization and specific formalisms (e.g. representing processing using Petri networks) or without any particular formalism (e.g. text, in certain requirements engineering methods).

DSS modeling is based on classic tools from conventional IT systems, particularly data modeling or knowledge (ontologies) modeling [BEL 13].

For data warehouses, *ad hoc* models have been designed, particularly at the logical level, to favor rapid query processing. The main model is the star schema, which places the fact table (the subject of analysis which we want to explore using a number of dimensions) in the center of the star and the dimensions at its points (e.g. geographical, time and product dimensions). The snowflake schema is based on the star schema, but it adds a hierarchical decomposition of its dimensions (by detailing, for example, the geographic dimension in a town, council region, county, etc.). The constellation schema combines a number of fact tables using the same dimensions.

2.2.1.3. *Way of organizing (approach and process)*

The *way of organizing* focuses on organizational approaches to the method, i.e. the lifecycle of the project. It is divided into the *way of working* (how to realize work) and the *way of controlling* (how to control the realization):

– the first approach directly relates to the description of the implementation of the method (the process) and particularly to the notion of the sequence of stages, each of the latter being described by a set of characteristics (objectives, input and output, processes, the players involved, resources used, risks, key success factors, etc.);

– the second approach concerns the decision cycle of the project (decision makers, basis on which the decision is made, types of possible decisions, reversibility of the decision, type of backtracking, etc.).

2.2.1.3.1. Types of approaches

IT system design has proposed different approaches, which were notably formalized by Boehm [BOE 88]. The processes of design methods for IT systems can be described based on the possibility they offer to easily backtrack to previous steps.

The oldest model, the *waterfall* model, only enables the user to backtrack to the previous step. Should a poor definition of requirements only be identified during the final phase and should the decision be made to correct it, they would have to "go back to" the first phase and redo all the steps. The *V* model reduces the rigidity of the waterfall model by introducing tests with varying ranges (unit test, integration test, validation test and acceptation test), which enable the user to backtrack to a previous step in the process. The *W* variant introduces the realization of a mock-up and is composed of 2 "Vs" side-by-side, the first concerning the realization of the mock-up and the tests conducted on it, and the second concerning the final system (production and tests).

The *spiral* model, also known as the *prototyping* model, adds new dimensions to the development of systems. In particular, it explicitly introduces risk management and constant evaluation by the users. The spiral's journey starts from the center and moves out (see Figure 2.2). The spiral moves from one round to another once a set of decisions has been made by those in charge of managing the project. This type of approach implies the possibility of precociously developing a prototype of the final system and then of modifying this prototype as many times as necessary and/or possible within the limits of the resources allocated to this project. This approach is particularly well suited to situations when it is difficult, or even impossible, to get hold of an accurate and exhaustive set of requirements, and/or when it is necessary for the users to be greatly involved so as to ensure the success of the project. This is specifically the case for DSS.

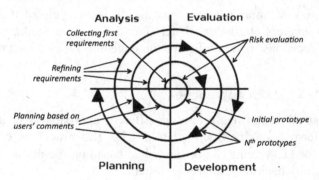

Figure 2.2. *Spiral model approach*

2.2.1.3.2. The phases of DSS design

The different phases of the DSS design approach are generally similar to the phases of conventional IT system design as follows in summary form:

1) requirements analysis and specifications (requirements engineering);

2) design (modeling: architecture, data, processing and HMI);

3) development;

4) tests and implementation;

5) managing the evolution of the system.

These phases can be realized following a waterfall model (rarely), a V or W model, or a spiral model (most frequently).

2.2.1.3.3. Sprague and Carlson's iterative approach

To design a DSS, Sprague and Carlson [SPR 82] advocated an iterative design approach, following the steps listed below. Their approach is still very relevant today:

1) choose an important subproblem with the user (which is small enough for its nature to be clear but crucial to the decision maker so they are motivated);

2) simultaneously analyze and develop a prototype: reduce the usual lifecycle to the minimum (analysis, design, implementation and evaluation) so that something useable can be produced very quickly;

3) use, evaluate and adjust the prototype with the user;

4) constantly evaluate the system.

To realize phases 2 and 3, they suggested using the ROMC approach, which is based on four steps, each of which focuses on a component of the DSS:

– representations (help conceptualize the problem to be solved, used to communicate and explain);

– operations (to analyze and handle the representations);

– memory aids (to support the use of representations and operations);

– control mechanisms (dividing actions between the user and the machine).

Each step results in a specific module of the DSS which is tested with the user so that, if necessary, the specifications can be reassessed.

Development in DSS today remains consistent with Sprague and Carlson's recommendations as it is mostly based on *agile* approaches, which follow spiral approaches and broadly use prototyping[6]. A key point concerning agile methods is that they place strong emphasis on interaction with the users (see the *Manifesto for Agile Software Development*[7]). Their weakness, however, is that they pay little attention to representations (the R of ROMC).

2.2.1.4. *Way of supporting (supports for implementing the method)*

All design methods for complex systems cause concrete problems for practical implementation. For instance, it is often said that many design methods for digital IT systems can only be correctly implemented by designers with extensive experience.

The *way of supporting* is dedicated to *supports for implementing* approaches. These supports are not a secondary part or appendix to a method, but rather they are an entire component in its own right.

Existing methods have identified a number of ways to support implementation. These supports can be categorized into four broad approaches, which are not mutually exclusive:

1) passing on necessary expertise to future designers, mostly by training or self-training (both require adjusted training supports);

2) providing guidance about the design process using standard documents, predefined sequence chains, checklists, examples, etc.;

3) making available software engineering tools (computer aided software engineering (CASE)) that include predefined models and functions, etc.;

---

6 It should be noted that agile methods are the direct descendants of the *rapid application development* (RAD) method, which emerged in the early 1990s [MAR 91].

7 http://agilemanifesto.org/.

4) providing already constituted elements or off-the-shelf components, to be used as they are, which can be of varied importance and levels of abstraction.

Whether they are specific or borrowed from conventional IT tools, methodological tools for DSS design benefit from training or self-training supports on the web as well as, often, from prototyping software. It should be noted that with regard to requirements engineering, very few methods propose examples with complete cases, with the exception of a number of methods from the world of research (see BIM).

2.2.1.5. Conclusion

Given that the requirements engineering phase determines the success of a DSS project (as will be seen later), the remainder of this chapter will be dedicated to the topic. First, requirements engineering will be discussed in general. Second, the specificities of requirements engineering for DSS and a number of examples of approaches will be presented.

2.2.2. Requirements engineering (not specific to DSS)

A very high number of IT projects are complete or partial failures[8]. The famous "Chaos" report from the Standish Group (which has been regularly updated since 1994) shows that in 2012 only 39% of projects were considered to be a success. Yet, the different design phases of an IT system or DSS are not all of the same level of importance regarding the successful completion of a project.

One of the crucial phases is the analysis of needs and requirements. For a long time this phase has been included within IT system engineering methods, of which it was the first step in the design process. In the 1990s, requirements engineering became a domain in

---

8 For a number of illustrative examples, see the *Catalogue of Catastrophe* available at: www.calleam.com/WTPF/?page_id=3.

its own right[9], when the critical character of the needs as well as the lack of methodological tools specific to need analysis became clear.

Requirements engineering as it will be described here was primarily developed for the design of conventional IT systems (and *not for DSS*, which causes problems which will be discussed later). Requirements engineering still bears the mark of this context today.

2.2.2.1. Justifying requirements engineering

In his famous article [BRO 86], Brooks vigorously affirmed the crucial character of requirement analysis:

> The hardest single part of building a software system is deciding precisely what to build. No other part of the conceptual work is as difficult as establishing the detailed technical requirements, including all the interfaces to people, to machines, and to other software systems. No part of the work so cripples the resulting systems if done wrong. No other part is more difficult to rectify later. Therefore, the most important function that the software builder performs for the client is the iterative extraction and refinement of the product requirements.

Several studies have since shown that the requirement analysis phase is the source of the majority of design errors in IT applications. Furthermore, it was established that if the requirement analysis phase occupies, on average, 2% of the total design time (and that its cost is insignificant compared to other phases such as development, implementation and testing), it is the cause of more than half of the errors committed during the system design.

Yet, the relative cost of correcting errors due to poor requirements analysis increases with the progress of the global process. Simply put, the later an error in needs and requirements analysis is detected, the more it costs to correct.

---

9 For a summary of the history of requirements engineering, see [HOO 08] which humorously describes the journey from the *client* to the *stakeholder* via the *user*.

To avoid these costly errors (as far as possible), requirements engineering sets itself the objective of improving the quality of the requirements needed for the development of a system.

2.2.2.2. Definitions of requirements engineering

All definitions of requirements engineering agree on the product of the requirements engineering process: what the system has to realize (the *what*) in contrast to the way in which it will be produced (the *how*).

Herlea's [HER 96] definition is representative of this consensus:

> Software requirements engineering is the process of determining what is to be produced in a software system. In developing a complex software system, the requirements engineering process has the widely recognized goal of determining the needs for, and the intended external behavior, of a system design.

Definitions of requirements engineering are generally, like Herlea's [HER 96], oriented to the output of the process (the requirements the system will have to meet) and give little or no indication about the nature of the needs and their context, nor about the expectations of the organization that will house the system.

That said, one of the oldest definitions of requirements engineering, Ross's [ROS 77], did tackle these questions. Used by numerous authors [VAN 00, LAP 05], this definition could be called visionary [MYL 00]:

> Requirements definition is a careful assessment of the needs that a system is to fulfill. It must say *why* a system is needed, based on current or foreseen conditions, which may be internal operations or an external market. It must say *what* system features will serve and satisfy this

context. And it must say *how* the system is to be constructed[10].

The question of *why*, i.e. the organization's objectives and their impact on the requirements the system has to meet, is the topic of a stream of research into requirements engineering: goal-driven requirements engineering which is particularly suitable for DSS design. This approach will be described in detail later in this chapter and illustrations from the domain of decision support will be provided.

2.2.2.3. *Needs or requirements?*

According to Rolland [ROL 11], needs "come from the stakeholders" and requirements are the "constraints imposed on the system to ensure the needs are met". It should be noted that in the majority of requirements engineering methods for DSS, most of the tools proposed concern "requirements". This is an expression of the hierarchy established between the *why* and the *what* (which gives the latter a dominant position over the former).

2.2.2.4. *Goal-driven requirements engineering*

Classic approaches to requirements engineering have centered on modeling the *what*; efforts have above all focused on modeling the relevant elements in the universe in question so as to produce a formalized conceptualization of what the system will be able to perform. Goal-driven requirements engineering has expanded its scope upstream by focusing on the organization's objective, the *why*, which the system must fulfill in cooperation with the agents concerned.

2.2.2.4.1. Definitions of the concept of goals

Antón [ANT 96] defines goals as follows:

> Goals are high-level objectives of the business, organization or system. They capture the reasons why a

---

10 The term "how" refers here to the constraints the systems has to respect and not to the technical solutions themselves.

system is needed and guide decisions at various levels within the enterprise.

Requirements are thus ways to realize goals. Upstream, requirements must therefore reflect the objectives of the organization. Downstream, requirements will determine design choices and potential technical solutions. It should be stressed that although in the majority of approaches goals are considered to *pre-exist* the requirements engineering process, they are not, however, considered as given or immediately available, but rather they require significant work to be extracted or elicited.

2.2.2.4.2. Goal-driven requirements engineering process

The standard activities of requirements engineering are generally categorized into four phases:

1) understanding the domain (early requirements) and extracting or eliciting the goals and requirements;

2) evaluating requirements, identifying conflicts and risks and negotiations between stakeholders to reach an acceptable solution;

3) specifying and documenting the features of the system to be built, realized with a degree of formalization that can vary a great deal;

4) final verification and validation of the requirements to produce the consolidated requirements.

These activities are organized within an incremental and strongly iterative process (within each phase and within the different phases), which can be represented with a spiral model.

We will now focus exclusively on the first phase, which is by a long way the most decisive for the success of a DSS project.

2.2.2.4.3. Understanding the domain and eliciting the goals and requirements

The activities in this phase are at the heart of requirements engineering. An understanding of the domain must enable the elicitation of goals and requirements to be prepared. This initial exploration of the organizational context within which the system being built must function constitutes the early requirements [FUX 04]. Early requirements thus make explicit the organization's broad strategic options, its broad objectives and the endogenous and exogenous constraints as well as, occasionally (although at the moment very rarely), its broad ethical values (see Chapter 4).

Next, the goals are understood. This task is widely recognized as being difficult [GAB 98, VAN 01], mostly because goals are often implicit and thus need to be elicited.

2.2.2.4.4. Modeling and formalizations

Modeling goals provide a means of communication between the managers of the organization and the system designers. Goals and requirements can be expressed in free natural language or using forms, as proposed by Pohl [POH 10]. They can also be represented with goal maps [ROL 99] or using models of varying degrees of formality. We are reminded by Rolland [ROL 11] that "requirements must be 'precise' which does not mean they must be 'formal'".

Certain models are oriented toward particular dimensions. The model associated with the $i*^{11}$ approach [YU 94], which is based on Goal-oriented Requirements Language (GRL) and is widely used in the community, provides a strategic dependency model: dependencies between actors, goals, tasks, etc.

These elements are used by requirements engineering for the development of a conventional IT system. Yet, requirements analysis for DSS and, more broadly, the design of the latter, presents a set of specificities that makes these methods inappropriate, at least in part. The next section is dedicated to requirements engineering for DSS.

---

11 i* (*iStar*) means *distributed intentionality*.

2.2.3. *Requirements engineering for DSS*

Although the importance of requirements analysis is now recognized in the domain of decision support [WIN 03], it has, as Golfarelli [GOL 09] stressed, been neglected for a long time and it has even been judged to be useful yet too costly [TIM 94]. Analyzing several data warehouse (DW) projects, List *et al.* [LIS 02] confirmed that many are relative failures in that they do not sufficiently meet the needs of their users. According to the authors, the main reason for this is the absence of requirements engineering methods that are specific to DSS design. The same statement is made about EIS [WAT 89, VOL 91, FRO 95] and even BI as a whole [BAR 10]. Similarly, in their study into the causes behind failed DSS, Arnott and Dodson [ARN 08a] stressed the importance of having well-defined requirements.

It should be noted that out of all decision support tools, the most numerous are still data-driven DSS. Out of these, data warehouses hold a special position [RAV 07]. However, as shown in a study by Arnott and Pervan [ARN 08b] into research in the domain of decision support, the field of data warehouses is, by its references, getting closer to the field of conventional IT systems (databases and data modeling) than the rest of the domain. Naturally, research on DW has, therefore, sought to use methods and modeling that exist in the field of conventional IT systems and adapt them where necessary. Consequently, the requirements engineering methods described here mostly concern DW development.

2.2.3.1. *The specificities of requirements engineering for DSS*

The specificities of requirements engineering for DSS design have been stressed by numerous authors in the domain. More than just simple differences between conventional IT systems and DSS, the difficulties that emerge are specific to decision support. These difficulties make requirements engineering much more complex for DSS than for conventional IT systems.

As mentioned above, requirements engineering is often neglected in DSS design and, particularly, in DW design [LIS 00]. Giorgini *et al.* [GIO 08] suggested three main reasons for this, which also describe the specificities of decision support projects:

1) they are long-term projects, consequently it is difficult to predict future needs;

2) decision-making processes are weakly structured, unstable and decision makers have a strong aversion to revealing them;

3) the needs expressed by the decision makers often concern information that is not available in the form requested and, therefore, often require complex processing.

These reasons relate to problems caused by, on the one hand, the system itself (takes a long time to build, based on information held by the organization and processing can be complex) and, on the other hand, aspects that are intrinsic to decision-making (needs that are difficult to predict, unstable decision-making process, difficulty and/or resistance of decision makers to explain their process or their needs). Only the latter will be discussed below.

2.2.3.1.1. Different needs depending on management levels

Given that decision-making processes differ depending on whether the decisions are well structured, weakly structured or unstructured, making a distinction between the different management levels (strategic, tactical and operational) seems to be essential if the requirements analysis for DSS development is to be a success. However, surprisingly, very few works on requirements engineering for DSS specifically deal with this topic.

Since 1971, Gorry and Scott Morton have indicated the specificities of the needs for each decision level. Likewise, Rockart, in his famous article [ROC 79] in which he popularized critical success factors (CSFs), stressed that the information needs of chief executive officers "are not as clearly determined as are those of many functional managers and first-line supervisors".

It should be noted that more recent authors in the domain of DSS have noticed the specific character of the needs of high-level decisions. With regard to strategic decisions, Sun and Liu [SUN 01] wrote:

> (…) the level of detail, granularity, format of presentation, and broad range of information type are unique for the applications at the strategic level.

2.2.3.1.2. The decision process: heuristic and unstable

For decisions supported by DSS (weakly structured or unstructured decisions dealing with problems that are sometimes undefined), the decision process, as described by Simon (see Chapter 1), is a strongly iterative heuristic process. As such, and even for decision situations that are in part already known, this process cannot be defined in advance. In the case of semi-structured decisions, short algorithmic fragments can be identified in the process, and some entities can already be relatively clearly structured by the decision maker. Nevertheless, the *whole* process cannot be set before the decision–making, and as such it is in the process' *nature* for it to be unstable and, particularly, unseizable.

2.2.3.1.3. Decision makers' difficulty and resistance to expressing their needs

A large number of authors have remarked that it is difficult to gather together the needs of users of DSS [GOL 09, WIN 03, LIS 00, BÖH 00, FRO 95]. A number of reasons for this are suggested, which involve different dimensions: communication between stakeholders, one shot decisions, the tacit nature of knowledge involved in decision-making and decision makers' resistance to expose their decision-making process. List *et al.* [LIS 00] mention the communication difficulties between system designers and users:

> A team of developers receives these descriptions, but they have trouble understanding the business terminology and find the description too informal/general to use for implementing the data warehouse system. The developers write their own system specification from a technical point of view. (…) This approach can easily result in a system that does not meet the requirements of the users

because often the users, the system analysts and developers don't speak the same language.

Needs relating to one shot decisions, which are growing in number, particularly in public decision-making, are difficult to understand [WIN 03, KLA 07].

More broadly, decision makers are akin to experts. It has been acknowledged that expert knowledge – specifically because it involves cognitive shortcuts the person is not/no longer aware of – requires specific work if it needs to be expressed or elicited. Finally, research on expert systems in the 1980s has produced countless examples of experts (participating in the design of a system) refusing to cooperate. The reasons given for this include: the fear of losing some of their power as well as the fear of being negatively judged for their professional practice, and challenged about it, which amounts to the fear of losing their job.

2.2.3.1.4. The difficulty of predicting needs

Although needs always evolve during the process of designing an IT system, during DSS design they can be profoundly modified [GOL 09]. The reason for this is twofold. First, the decision maker, who at the beginning of the process was unable to clearly understand which information they could obtain, gains an increasingly clearer understanding as the project moves forward. Second, in the context of the economic environment described in Chapter 1, the organization's strategy can move in a very different direction within a relatively short period of time, which may be less than the duration of a DSS design project.

The difficulty of predicting needs can be exacerbated by differences of decision makers' opinions about what the future of the enterprise and its environment will be (list of future events as well as the interpretation of these events). Financialization strategies, by concentrating the decision-making power in the hands of the senior management by imposing short-term horizons and organizational changes at a very fast pace, have left some managers feeling more confused and finding it difficult to envisage a now illegible future, on which they do not feel capable to act.

2.2.3.2. *Types of requirements engineering approaches for DSS*

Requirements engineering approaches for decision support, particularly for data-driven DSS, are often classified into three broad categories, depending on whether they are data-driven, requirement-driven or goal-driven.

2.2.3.2.1. Data-driven approaches

Data-driven or supply-driven approaches, which are bottom-up approaches, start by analyzing the data available in the IT system and then the future user selects, from within this finite set, the data that are relevant to them. List *et al.* [LIS 02] said:

> The approach ignores the needs of data warehouse users
> *a priori.* Company goals and user requirements are not
> reflected at all. User needs are integrated in the second
> cycle.

In this approach, users' needs take on a secondary role [GIO 08], and there is a risk that the system produced will not meet the real needs of decision makers. This risk is particularly high for decision makers at the strategic level [GOL 09] whose decisions require complex indicators. This type of approach does, however, remain the least costly of the three in terms of both time and financial resources. As such, it is the most widely used approach today.

2.2.3.2.2. Requirement-driven approaches

User-driven, demand-driven or requirement-driven approaches consider that only decision makers can define their needs and, therefore, start by analyzing decision makers. Like data-driven approaches, requirement-driven approaches are bottom-up. One of the risks of these approaches is that decision makers are not always capable of defining their expectations because they do not have a good knowledge of the information available and they find it difficult to imagine the options the system could offer them [WIN 03]. Moreover, it is implied that users know and understand the global objectives of the organization and have a shared view of it. However, these hypotheses are far from being well established [MIN 94, GUO 06].

2.2.3.2.3. Goal-driven approaches

The third approach is goal-driven. These approaches are very similar to goal-driven approaches for conventional IT systems and are top-down. They first elicit the high-level goals (the strategy) of the organization with the senior management, and then divide them into a range of subgoals spanning all levels until the level of the decision makers (future users of the system is built). These approaches are particularly useful when the decision makers (future users of the system) do not have a clear understanding of the organization's strategy.

Mixed approaches, combining two or even three of the three types of approaches, exist [GUO 06, RAV 07].

It should be noted that the methods used in the first two types of approaches (data-driven and requirement-driven) do not generally include the "way of thinking" and, therefore, do not make explicit their presuppositions about what constitutes a decision, organization management, etc.

This book will not discuss data-focused approaches, as they do not adapt well to weakly structured or unstructured decisions (that are the subject of decision support), and user-focused approaches, which we consider too restrictive as they do not integrate the needs of the organization as a whole. We will, therefore, focus exclusively on goal-driven approaches, which we believe offer a promising future.

2.2.3.3. Goal-driven approaches

This section presents a number of goal-driven requirements engineering approaches to DSS design. These approaches have taken inspiration, sometimes directly, from approaches developed for conventional IT systems. Therefore, they use the concepts and principles presented above.

This section does not aim to be exhaustive: the methods presented here were selected because they represent goal-driven approaches. In addition, the focus here is on the analysis of early requirements.

2.2.3.3.1. Critical success factors

The CSF approach does not align itself with goal-driven engineering, but it does, like the latter, focus on determining and breaking down the organization's high-level goals and can be very useful for identifying early requirements.

Rockart [ROC 79] was one of the first researchers to focus on the information requirements of enterprises' senior management, i.e. the support needs for strategic or tactical management. According to Rockart, a major problem is that an enterprise's director receives a large amount of information which is not very relevant.

He, therefore, suggested analyzing director's needs by using Daniel's [DAN 61] CSF. Rockart described CSF as follows:

> Critical success factors thus are, for any business, the limited number of areas in which results, if they are satisfactory, will ensure successful competitive performance for the organization. (...) As a result, the critical success factors are areas of activity that should receive constant and careful attention from management.

Like in goal-driven requirements engineering, the general goals of the organization must first be determined and then they would be specified by identifying the CSF that will guarantee their best chance of success.

2.2.3.3.2. The GRAnD approach

In the GRAnD approach, Giorgini *et al.* [GIO 08] adjust the Tropos method (based on the conceptual framework of *i**) to DW design. Two modeling approaches are identified:

– the organizational context that has to cover all the stakeholders;

– the decision-making process of the decision maker(s), the future users of the system.

New concepts are added to *i**, all of which are closely linked to the specificities of DW, namely: *fact* (set of events that occur when a goal is met), *dimension* (the properties of facts, which correspond to one possible analysis approach for the achievement of a goal) and *measures* (digital property of a fact that describes a quantitative aspect that is relevant to decision-making).

It should be noted, however, that the Tropos method could have been used to analyze the upstream requirements of DSS other than the DW. Perini and Susi [PER 04] therefore applied Tropos to understand the domain of integrated production in agriculture in northern Italy in the context of DSS design intended to support technicians and farmers. All the players, their interactions and goals were modelized.

2.2.3.3.3. The CADWE method

Gam [GAM 08] used the conceptual tools developed in the CREW project [ROL 99], and further research was carried out by Rolland's team to create the *computer-aided data warehouse engineering* (CADWE) method that analyzes requirements for data warehouses. The work is a complete requirements engineering method, but we will only discuss the part that describes goals and requirements.

The concept of *functional requirements* from requirements engineering for conventional IT systems is replaced here by the concept of *information requirements*. Like for conventional IT systems, requirements emerge from either the intentional level or the operational level. Requirements from the intentional level relate to the strategic and tactical management levels, in the perspective of a development of strategic requirements toward information requirements (called *operationalizable* requirements). Information requirements operationalized in system requirements constitute the operational level (in the sense of the CADWE method).

This method makes a considerable effort to deal with the strategic and tactical levels. However, it lacks a management model that clearly characterizes, on the one hand, the objectives, the action variables and the different types of indicators, and, on the other hand, the different management levels. This situation appears to be very common in the literature of requirements engineering for DW (as well as for GRAnD). This absence has a negative impact on the clarity and effectiveness of the different tools of the CADWE method (list of strategic goals, map of strategic objectives, map of tactical objectives and list of information requirements).

These comments can be assimilated to the research of a number of analysts in the domain who stress the gap between BI and the enterprise's strategy. In 2009, a report by the Gartner Group entitled "Overcoming the Gap between Business Intelligence and Decision Support" [SAL 09] went further still:

> Although the promise of better decision making is a top driver of business intelligence (BI) and performance management investment, information generated by BI systems and other decision inputs are rarely linked to business decisions and outcomes.

A similar comment was made by Arnott and Dodson [ARN 08a] who stated that the absence of a clearly established link with the enterprise's strategy was one of the causes of failed DSS projects. A Gartner analysis [BIT 11] confirms that these problems are still common in the overwhelming majority of organizations.

In our opinion, these weaknesses in DSS projects can largely be attributed to failings in requirements engineering.

2.2.3.3.4. The business intelligence model

Starting from these observations, recent research is focusing more closely on the global architecture of the organization's management and on the *content* of decisions. This research is, therefore, putting right some of the absences we identified in the previous approaches.

One of the most completed works is unquestionably the BIM. The BIM derives from the observation that there is a gap between requirements at the strategic level and DSS [BAR 10]:

Unfortunately, there is a huge cognitive gap between a requirements view of a strategic initiative articulated in terms of business goals, processes, and performance on one hand, and an implementation view of BI monitoring articulated in terms of databases, networks, and computational processing.

To bridge this gap, Barone *et al.* and Horkoff *et al.* [BAR 10, HOR 14, BAR 14] suggest bringing together, on the one hand, tried and tested models from the domain of management and, on the other hand, techniques from conceptual modeling and goal-driven requirements engineering (in this case *i**). The method proposed by the authors, and which goes beyond mere requirements engineering, is composed of three basic elements:

– the BIM, which represents the needs concerning the strategy and its development;

– the *conceptual integration model* (CIM), which represents a view of organizational data implemented in the data warehouse;

– a structure bringing together the BIM and the CIM, with enterprise dashboards connecting both levels.

The BIM enables users to conceptualize their strategies and actions in a language that is familiar to them and which includes the concepts of actor, directive, intention, event, situation, indicator, influence and process. The BIM was designed by combining recognized management approaches, such as the business motivation model (BMM[12]), the strengths, weaknesses, opportunities, threats (SWOT) matrix and Kaplan and Norton's [KAP 96] Balanced Scorecard[13] (mentioned in Chapter 1). Using and supplementing the concepts of *i**, Barone *et al.* [BAR 10] clearly identify the objectives, projects or processes that enable them to be implemented[14] and the indicators that measure their achievement. Figure 2.3 shows a simplified

---

12 See http://www.omg.org/spec/BPMN/2.0/.

13 See Chapter 1, section 1.3.4.

14 In Mélése's terminology [MÉL 72], these projects and processes correspond to action variables (see Chapter 1, section 1.3.2).

representation of an (fictional) enterprise's strategy according to the BIM model.

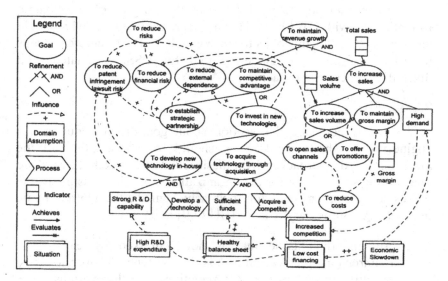

Figure 2.3. *Example of BIM modeling*
(http://ww.cs.toronto.edu/~jm/bim/)

The CIM combines three levels: a conceptual model of the DW, a physical model of the DW and a system corresponding between the two models.

A complete engineering tool is associated with the method[15]. The method has been applied to several cases, primarily in the domain of health.

By focusing on an organization's management structure, by expressing its strategy and breaking down the latter into subobjectives, and furthermore by focusing on the content of these objectives (notably via four types of strategic objectives from the *Balanced Scorecard*), the BIM makes up for some of the insufficiencies we identified in the previous approaches. Information needs seem,

---

15 The tool is demonstrated at www.cs.toronto.edu/~jm/bim.

however, to be relatively undifferentiated (mostly concerning indicators and only performance indicators).

In recent developments, BIM was the subject of a semantic formalization with OWL[16], which enables reasoning like "what would happen if...?" or "is this objective achievable?". BIM, therefore, tends to become a complete modeling tool for DSS, associated with diversified processing capacities.

2.2.3.3.5. Conclusion

To briefly conclude this section about goal-driven requirements engineering methods for DSS, it should be stressed that all the aforementioned approaches hypothesize that the stakeholders share one and the same vision for the organization's missions, its goals, the tactics to be implemented for their achievement, the metrics to be used, etc. As Burgemeestre *et al.* [BUR 09] remark:

> An important issue that is not addressed by early requirements methods like *i** is the existence of overlap or differences in the interpretations of the various stakeholders. Much work in requirements engineering implicitly assumes that mental models of the task and domain are shared among stakeholders. In practice however, this assumption is not always warranted.

A number of other authors appeal for the different perspectives that may coexist within one organization to be taken into account. In addition, the majority of these methods consider the strategy to be *defined*, accessible if not given.

Chapter 3 will deal with these topics, which are linked to the worldviews of the different stakeholders in a DSS project.

---

16 OWL: Web Ontology Language is, as the name suggests, a language that represents ontologies (form of representation of knowledge in the form of a structured set of concepts), intended to be used online.

Conclusion: key points for DSS design

Decisions supported by DSS

Historic definitions of DSS stress that they are intended to support weakly structured or unstructured decisions, which mostly correspond to the tactical and strategic management levels. However, it must be said that very few market tools are capable of supporting strategic decisions or even complex tactical decisions.

What the history of DSS teaches us

Like many fields in IT, after an initial period that was open to pluridisciplinarity, the majority of research has focused on technical tools, to the detriment of the purpose of DSS, which are designed to accompany the organization as it evolves. It is worth stressing again that the main issue of decision support is the decision, which is an element of organizational life. Research on DSS must always be conscious of the need to understand the sense of the decisions and their role within the organization.

Business intelligence tools and criticism about BI

BI has produced numerous DSS-specific tools. The most mature concerns data-driven DSS (data warehouse). Big Data represents a rupture in decision support, not from the technical point of view, but via the potentially considerable impact that could be the result of their use.

A recurrent criticism leveled at DSS is that they do not respond to needs, that they are disconnected from the enterprise's strategy and that they are incapable of really supporting strategic decision-making.

DSS design methods

Unlike the domain of IT systems, the domain of DSS has produced very few universal methods. The majority of these methods remain linked to tools. Out of the components of one method, the first (*way of thinking*), which sets out the broad views of the entities in question, the theory on which the method is based and the epistemological perspective to which it subscribes, is generally absent from DSS engineering methods.

The importance of requirements engineering in DSS design

Requirements engineering has been neglected from DSS design for many years. This type of engineering is particularly difficult to conduct due to the specificities of the decision-making. For the same reason, requirements engineering methods for conventional IT systems are unsuitable. The DSS domain has produced very few requirements engineering methods, but this situation is currently changing.

Requirements engineering is vital for the success of a DSS project as the role of the DSS within the organization is identified at this stage as well as, of course, the needs of the decision makers to which it will respond. The first phase, early requirements analysis, determines the rest of the process; specifically, it sets the broad worldviews that will structure the entire DSS.

As will be seen in the next chapter, these worldviews determine in large part the content of the decisions made. It is, therefore, important to preserve their diversity. Chapter 4 will deal with this necessity.

The Influence of DSS on Decision-Making and Associated Risks

Introduction: is the freedom of the decision maker an illusion?

The domain of information technology (IT) systems like the domain of decision support systems (DSS) makes the (unwritten) assumption, in the overwhelming majority of its work, that these technologies are neutral and therefore cannot influence the way in which tasks are performed or decisions are taken. Yet, research in other disciplines has shown that defining the problem, which is an essential phase in the decision process, can be largely determined by a set of factors, including DSS.

The purpose here is not to deny the positive aspects of DSS which are, quite rightly, widely recognized, but to highlight how these systems can influence decision-making, for the most part, in an invisible way. For us, this reflection is vital, particularly from the perspective of engineering these systems. In the design methods, it concerns the *way of thinking*, the essential nature of which has already been stressed. This poses not only the question of democracy (within organizations, at the level of the State and even society), but also questions about the economy and consequently society.

This chapter will, therefore, seek to understand what can limit the freedom of decision-making, what can orient, influence and hamper the choice made by one or more person(s).

Section 3.1 will explore the main factors which, in our opinion, influence decision-making. It should be noted that out of these factors, we will not discuss types of organization or management methods, the psychological traits of the decision maker or group dynamics. The influence factors that we have identified fall into two categories: endogenous or exogenous. Endogenous factors are linked to the cognitive functioning of decision makers, which in part drive the decision, and in particular the perspective to which the decision maker subscribes, which is itself determined by their worldviews. Exogenous factors are management technologies, which include the information system (IS), the IT system and the DSS, which orient reasoning. The performative character of these systems will be highlighted. Big Data will be specifically discussed, which due to their huge volumes produce a massive "effect of reality". We will finally pause on a usage of IT systems and DSS which is claimed to be a "persuasive technology".

As the factors guiding decision-making will have then been described, section 3.2 will question the risks that their influence causes to the organization and, sometimes, to society as a whole. Error-related risks (in data and calculations) as well as the more significant risks of potential confusion with the real (of an infinite complexity and its) coding, which is by definition very simplified, will therefore be tackled. The feedback produced by the performative effects of the IS, IT system and DSS also carries risks to the extent that implementing certain indicators may lead to the opposite result of the one being sought. Finally, the serious epistemological problems that accompany Big Data could lead to major risks.

3.1. Factors influencing decision-making

As described in Chapter 1 (section 1.2.1), in Simon's intelligence, design, choice (IDC) decision process, it is in the *intelligence* phase that the need to make a decision is identified and then the *representation* of the perceived problem is built.

After noticing that the first part of this sentence ("What brings (and should bring) problems to the head of the agenda?") is poorly understood, Simon *et al.* [SIM 86] commented:

> The way in which problems are represented has much to do with the quality of the solutions that are found. (…) The representation or "framing" of problems is even less well understood than agenda setting. Today's expert systems make use of problem representations that already exist. But major advances in human knowledge frequently derive from new ways of thinking about problems.

The second part of the *intelligence* phase, the way in which the problem is represented, will therefore greatly influence the rest of the decision process, as Paradice [PAR 08] confirmed:

> The alternatives from which a decision maker may be able to choose are integrally tied to the assumptions made about the problem situation.

This is particularly true for weakly or unstructured decisions and undefined problems ("wicked problems", see Chapter 1, section 1.2.4). The world is currently facing undefined problems in ever-increasing numbers; it is even impossible to tell the formulation of the problem apart from its solution, as the fathers of the concept of "wicked problems" Rittel and Webber [RIT 73] have shown:

> The formulation of a wicked problem *is* the problem! The process of formulating the problem and of conceiving a solution (or re-solution) are identical, since every specification of the problem is a specification of the direction in which a treatment is considered.

It is, therefore, essential to understand which factors have an impact on the identification of a problem and its formulation.

Successively, we will discuss factors internal to the process or the decision maker (sections 3.1.1–3.1.3) and then external factors (sections 3.1.4–3.1.10). It should be noted that we will not deal with dynamics within groups, which play an undisputable role, whether decision-making is collective or individual. Purely psychological aspects will also not be discussed.

3.1.1. *The three types of problem-solving error*

This section will explore the types of error in problem solving, the importance of perspectives and, finally, the role of decision makers' mental representations.

Simon assimilates the decision-making process to problem solving. Errors can be made during problem solving.

Statistics recognizes two types of error. In type I errors, a hypothesis is said to have been validated, when in fact it has not. This type of error is known as excessive credulity. Type II errors express the opposite mistake. In this case, hypotheses are mistakenly rejected. This second type of error can be seen as an expression of excessive skepticism. These two types of error occur in the context of an already defined problem, for which the variables have been identified. They, therefore, relate to structured decisions. Mitroff and Linstone [MIN 93] supplement this typology with a third type. A type III error regards the *definition of the problem itself*[1] and, therefore, concerns weakly structured or unstructured decisions. This type of error is described as *solving the wrong problem* (*precisely*). It should be noted that Mitroff then added a fourth type of error [MIT 10]. A type III error occurs when we solve the wrong problem *unintentionally*. A type IV error consists of solving the wrong problem *intentionally* and imposing an incorrect definition of the problem on the other players.

In DSS design, taking into account a number of perspectives (and not only the technical perspective, for example) by multiplying the

---

1 The notion of a type III error was first proposed by Howard [HOW 68] (cited by [MIT 97]).

views of the situation, the end purposes, the constraints, etc., enables type III errors to be reduced. Type IV errors, on the other hand, can only be reduced if the organization in question functions in a democratic way enabling the basis on which a decision has been made to be questioned.

3.1.2. The role of perspectives in problem formulation

The notion of the multiplicity of perspectives can be considered in a restrictive way: at the level of the organization and of its different activities. In this case, we move toward viewpoints as they are considered in the world of conventional IT systems, i.e. mostly *departmental* viewpoints [CAH 04]. Faced with a problematic situation, managers of the different departments in the enterprise do not generally spontaneously build the same representation, rather their representation is linked to their activity (research and development (R&D), marketing, finance, production, etc.). The significant objects for each department, as well as the concepts they use, always differ, at least in part.

In the context of decision support, the notion of perspective is at a higher level than that of the departmental viewpoints and is positioned on a plane that could be called paradigmatic.

Mitroff and Linstone [MIT 93] identify three perspectives that influence problem formulation, which are grouped into the technical, organizational and personal (TOP) model. Each of these perspectives arises from a paradigm (value system and ways of reasoning) that is specific to it. While making a decision, one decision maker may express a number of perspectives, which have varying degrees of importance. However, it is recognized that a decision must be made (a problem must be set) according to one main perspective (though it is not easy to predict which before the start of the decision process).

The *scientific/technical perspective* corresponds to looking for rationality. The situation is analyzed to produce the list of rational solutions to the problem.

The *organizational (or systemic) perspective* looks to analyze the problem and in particular the effects of the possible solutions, by considering the whole system in question. The definition of this system can be very extensive.

The *personal perspective* then called the *interpersonal/social perspective* analyzes the problem from the point of view of an individual's relationship with others.

The final perspective (added to the three perspectives of the TOP model), called the *existential perspective* by Mitroff [MIT 97], concerns an individual's deepest values, the sense they give to their life, ethics, etc. The problem is, therefore, analyzed in view of these fundamental values.

Other authors have proposed supplementing these perspectives by new dimensions. When proposing a "new paradigm for decision making", Courtney [COU 01] added the *ethical* and *esthetic* dimensions, which were taken up by Chae *et al.* [CHA 05]. Chapter 4 will discuss the ethical perspective.

3.1.3. *Mental representations, worldviews and beliefs*

Each of the aforementioned perspectives belongs to a more general context: the decision maker's *worldviews*, which could be called their *beliefs* (in the sense of something, in the latter case, whose truth cannot be proved by scientific methods[2]) about the composition of the environment in which they operate and its state. Beliefs influence both parts of the *intelligence* phase.

Recognizing the problematic character of a situation, the first part of the *intelligence* phase, therefore, depends directly on the mental representation of the decision maker(s). Famous examples from history show that, although equipped with all the necessary information, decision makers were not able to understand the gravity of a situation as it was too distant from what they could

_____

2 For more information about the different regimes of beliefs, see [ATL 14].

mentally conceive. Spy Sorge warned Stalin about the German invasion, but Stalin was unable to accept the idea of Hitler's "betrayal" and, therefore, did not organize any defense for his country. Likewise, the Central Intelligence Agency (CIA) should have had enough data to predict the September 11 attacks and all sorts of authorities were warned by a number of experts of the imminent financial crash before September 2008, but in both cases, decisions matching the (high)-risk level were not taken.

The aforementioned perspectives are determined by these worldviews.

The *scientific/technical perspective* relates to rationality, but rationality is multiple and each of its forms is strictly linked to the representations of the world in which it exists. By way of example, let us consider a medical patient. A "Western" doctor's diagnosis of this patient will not be expressed in the same terms as the diagnosis made by a practitioner of traditional Chinese medicine. The representation of the human body, the malfunction of this body and the means to restore it to a state of health will be very different. Western medicine views a body as a sum of organs (each of which is considered to be relatively autonomous from the others) and that the state of health is the state of health of a given organ; Chinese medicine primarily considers the flows of energy moving around the body and views the state of health as being a state of balanced energies.

Rational thought is based on existing categories, though it also produces new categories. Yet, in several disciplines, authors have shown that natural classifications do not exist and that categories are built for a specific purpose and/or are produced by doxa effects[3]. For illustration purpose, we can quote [HAC 06] for scientific classifications, [BOL 87] for the category of executives, [DES 98] for public statistics and, more globally, [RAS 06, RAS 04] for the social character of semantic classes or "the impact of doxa norms" on discourse.

---

3 From the Greek δόξα: opinion.

The *organizational perspective* takes into account the entire system concerned. Nevertheless, definitions of the system in question, its mission and consequently its boundaries can be different and contrasting. Following Friedman [FRI 70], a decision maker may therefore consider that the enterprise has "one and only one" mission: "to use its resources and engage in activities designed to increase its profits". This decision maker will then establish a hierarchy of stakeholders in which only shareholders are allowed to take part in defining the enterprise's mission. Another decision maker from the same enterprise might believe that the mission of the enterprise (of which they are part) is to produce and sell goods and services that are useful to society (with the objective of making profit) and will thus include in their representation of the system a large set of stakeholders, some of whom are external to the legal entity in question.

The problem analyzed by the *interpersonal* perspective is clearly the representation the decision maker creates of relationships between people. Does the decision maker consider the way people relate as based on competition, consistent with the figure of *homo œconomicus* (calculating and egotistical) or, in contrast, does the decision maker put emphasis on trust between players?

Existential, ethical and *esthetic* perspectives are based on representations of what is good, fair, beautiful, etc., which vary a great deal from one culture to another and from one individual to another. For example, the representation of the individual's freedom of expression in society is noticeably different in different countries or cultures.

We have thus far discussed aspects that are internal to the decision-making process or the decision maker and which have an influence on the formulation of the problem and, therefore, on decision-making. However, there are also *external* elements that have a strong influence on the representation that an organization or a decision maker creates of a situation or a problem.

3.1.4. *The influence of management technologies*

DSS cannot be dissociated from a specific complex technology, IT, and more broadly digital technology. This section will question the impact technologies in general have on problem formulation and taking into account the different perspectives. The sections below will focus more specifically on IS.

Technologies used for the operation and management of organizations, whether management methods, management tools or IS, have for a long time been (and are often still) believed to be neutral, simple tools that serve decision makers and unable to cast an influence.

However, since 1983, in his pioneering work, Berry stresses the role of what he calls *management tools*:

> This is how instruments like simple ratios, classifications, selection criteria, IT or non-IT management systems become the elements of an invisible technology whose harmful effects are all the more implacable since we let them play in the shadows.

> (...) management tools are often decisive elements with regard to structuring the real, producing choices and behaviors that escape the grasp of humans, sometimes of their conscience.

The author describes the main effects of these management technologies:

> (...) reduction of complexity, implementation of automatic decision making, division of vigilance, regulation of social relationships and maintenance of coherence

He concludes "this is the stewardship which is in charge and not the willpower". He advises paying attention "less to the stated intentions and the visible exercise of power than to the procedures and tools that have been concretely implemented", by analyzing the logics the latter induce. It should be noted that the analysis of management tools and their impact on the organization is one of the main topics of research in the domain of the sociology of management[4]. Among these, *machines of management*[5], IS and IT systems play a central role.

3.1.5. *IS: performative systems*

IS, in the sense of the term we described in the introduction of this book, are systems that formalize representations. The IS of an organization can, therefore, be assimilated to its *language*, i.e. an ability to take stock of the "real" in a form that can be shared by a community of players. Through this language, IS structure the way an organization's players operate and as such have a *normative* character.

However, beyond this, through the norms and the values they express, IS have an *instituting* or *performative*[6] character. What is defined in/by the IS automatically acquires a status of "reality" and enables and even systematically brings about decision-making and action.

For instance, some illnesses, when they appear in an official classification, bring about a specific pharmaceutical offer (see the debates about the new classification of mental illness in the United States, which it was claimed *created* mental health problems[7]).

In the domain of public action, the designation, in classifications, of a given sector (for instance, the "biomedical" sector) makes

---

4 In France, see RT30 (Réseau Thématique) of the Association Française de Sociologie =: www.afs-socio.fr/RT30.

5 Girin [GIR 93] uses Marx's distinction between tools and machines, humans using tools and machines using humans.

6 We are using this term in a broader sense than that originally used by Austin and we understand it as the capacity to impose, by way of language, the existence of an object.

7 An article from *Le Monde* dated 13/05/2013 and entitled "Psychiatrie: DSM-5, le manuel qui rend fou" [Psychiatry: DSM-5, the manual that makes you mad].

initiatives focused on enterprises said to belong to this sector conceivable. In contrast, the absence of a designation of a sector makes it *invisible* to public decision makers [SAL 13a]. Not naming, therefore, equates to not being able to consider. In the Midi-Pyrénées region in France, it has for a long time been the case that onboard systems was not included in classifications used by the region and as such was not the object of any specific action. The manufacturers concerned were very unhappy about this and increased lobbying to get their domain recognized by the region.

In enterprises, the very limited sets of indicators used to represent the operation of the whole organization bring about decisions and actions aimed exclusively at improving these indicators. The specificities of indicators will be discussed in the next section.

More broadly, Desrosières [DES 03], when describing the objects of public accounting, shows that "quantification does not reflect reality, but rather, in contrast, it helps shape it, transform it and even create it". This involves the performative aspect of classifications, which Boydens [BOY 99] reminds us are always "historically and socially situated" and have "performative effects [that] are inscribed in the thus standardized real". Also present here is the specific effect of Hofstadter's "strange loops" which bring together information and decision-making, as information forms the organization that forms it [LEM 91].

3.1.6. *Indicators: an extreme case of reduced complexity*

The current management of organizations – whether public or private – is very widely (and increasingly so) based on regular quantitative measurements: indices ("abstracts of the truth" according to Berry) and indicators ("abstracts of the good")[8]. This section will focus on indicators.

The quantitative character of indicators certainly contributes toward their image of technicality, neutrality and, beyond this, *truth*.

---

8 For definitions of the terms *index* and *indicator*, see Chapter 1 (section 1.3.3).

Yet, quantification is not, in any way, a simple process and does not lend itself to any discussion, as Desrosières [DES 12] showed when he wrote:

> The verb *to quantify* in its active form (*to make* into numbers), presupposes that a series of prior equivalence conventions has been developed and made explicit, involving comparisons, negotiations, compromises, translations, inscriptions, encodings, codified and replicable procedures and calculations leading to numerization. The measurement, in the strict sense, comes afterward, as the rule-based implementation of these conventions.

The development of the "prior equivalence conventions", which Desrosières describes as what could be called a social process, unfortunately remains for the most part implicit. Development is, therefore, conducted from an exclusively technical perspective which ignores or denies the *issues of representation* which are at the origin of these conventions. IT systems' ability to automatically generate indicators (and indices) further emphasizes this fact.

At the European level, the "Lisbon strategy" imposed economic objectives about the *employment rate* to replace objectives about the *unemployment rate*. This new indicator automatically directs public policies toward improving the former rather than the latter, and the evolution of this rate in turn reinforces the direction of the actions. Yet, with regard to calculating employment rate, a person is considered to be employed if they have one or more jobs, regardless of how many hours they spend working. As such, a person who works for 4 h a week is considered to be employed. The employment rate (which does not equate to full-time work) can, therefore, increase even when the number of full-time workers is falling. The unemployment rate measures the number of people who declare they are looking for work. The representation of the economic health of a country, therefore, differs depending on which of these two indicators is used[9].

---

9 For more information about this, see various papers by Salais (e.g. [SAL 04]).

With regard to the role of IS in public management, Le Galès [LEG 05] showed that overhauls to the state structure in the UK were only possible due to "the development of a very large information system" and talks of a real "industry of the indicator".

In the life of organizations, the widespread use of indicators – as the only way to conduct evaluations – leads to notable performative effects. In line with the maxim "tell me how you're going to evaluate me and I'll tell you how I'll behave", countless cases have been observed when activity is no longer driven by the objective to be reached or the mission to be realized, but rather by the sole goal of improving evaluation indicators. These feedback effects will be discussed later (section 3.2.3.1).

3.1.7. *IT: a technology of representations*

In our opinion, IT is inherently a technology that *produces signs*, i.e. it produces "equivalents" of the universe being considered in the form of a specific code. It, therefore, represents certain static or dynamic elements of the real world, enabling them to be stored, processed and communicated. Through their operations, they generate elements in the real world (e.g. the "click" of the mouse, standardized modeling languages in IT engineering, the concept of opening a window on a screen, etc.).

With regard to the static elements of the represented universe, these "equivalents" are usually designated with the terms *data* and *information*, although the difference between these terms is not always made. For the meantime, we will use the term *data,* but later we will discuss the, in our opinion, fundamental distinction that must be drawn between the concepts of data, information and knowledge (see section 3.2.4.3.3).

Data, collected from the real world by various means, or generated by technology itself, are coded in *digital* form (binary). Data are processed by a limited number of logical and arithmetical operations which are also coded in digital form. Digitized data can lead to simple or complex calculations, be grouped, categorized and aggregated, and thereby produce new data. Likewise, the basic operations of a processor can be combined to form more complex instructions organized in programming languages, which, in turn, enable the development of generic tools (generally software engineering tools) used to produce new tools or applications.

IT, therefore, causes layers of successive representations to be stacked up. Via different types of processing applied to data and operations available at its level, each layer produces the next representation, which is then considered to be the basis on which to apply new types of processing, which will produce the next layer and so on. IT is, therefore, a technology of representations (in the plural), which take the form of screens, filters and reductions of the complexity of the real in question.

Yet, though IT produces elements of the real that are specific to it, IT systems, intensely used in a broad set of professional or private activities, are as a whole an undeniably important component of the *real* in the life of individuals and organizations and are inextricably linked to the components of the tangible or intangible real that these technologies represent. Consequently, an increasingly larger number of employees work exclusively not with objects that they can concretely handle, but rather with the digital representation of these objects that their organization's IT system offers/imposes on them. The same is true for the players with whom they interact (clients, suppliers, subcontractors, etc.). Simultaneously, clients who have been "put to work"[10] order products online, which are finally delivered to them in a tangible world, without having had any contact with the employees who design, produce, check, commercialize or send the products.

This results in a totally remarkable "effect of reality" in the use of IT systems. The succession of screens between the palpable real and the digital representation with which a person interacts is, at best, experienced as one screen (which supposedly faithfully reflects reality), but is most often ignored.

---

10 See [TIF 13].

The aforementioned performativity of IS is thus very strongly reinforced in their digital part. Going further still, Walsham [WAL 11] notes that these systems also reflect values:

> Computer-based information systems and the related discourse on IS strategy reflect norms and values concerning the individual, the organization, and the broader society at large (...)

If we remember that the representation of the problem plays a decisive role in decision-making, then we must specifically question the consequences of the use of DSS.

3.1.8. *DSS: support and/or constraint?*

DSS are a specific component of IT systems which support, in particular, the definition of the organization's management system (defining missions, strategic axes, different levels of objectives, control and action methods, etc.). The IT system gives an implicit representation of the organization's missions, especially through:

– objects and their characteristics that the system codes (with the related performative effects) and, conversely, objects or characteristics that it does not code (and which are thus invisible and inaccessible);

– indicators, which are very aggregated representations of what counts and what has meaning to the organization.

DSS use the data available in the IT system alongside, though in a still relatively limited way (with the exception of certain applications of Big Data), the support of external data. A certain representation of the organization, of its relationships with its environment, its real and desired trajectory, of what is a successful operation, etc., as it is coded in the IT system, is therefore actually (and most often *invisibly*) imposed on the decision makers using DSS.

Meredith and Arnott [MER 03] therefore believe that DSS limit the independence of decision makers by imposing structures on their thought-processes, by directing their attention toward this or that piece of information:

> Another distinguishing feature of DSS *[decision support systems]* development and use is the impact of the system upon the cognitive strategies and structures of the user. Whilst an operational system has some impact upon its users in terms of understanding and task approach, the degree to which a DSS has an impact on the user's cognitive strategies and structures is much greater due to the uncertain, unstructured nature of the task.

It should be noted that unstructured (tactical and strategic) decisions, which the above quotation concerns, have the biggest impact on the organization. These decisions are connected to *innovation* (which regards all the operations in an enterprise: product definition, manufacturing processes, market segmentation, methods, organization, IS, etc.).

3.1.9. *Big Data: a massive "effect of reality"*

Big Data due to the number of dimensions retained, their very large volumes, the historicization of data and their quick update time, want to give the image of an exhaustive and neutral digitization of the *totality of the real*. Processing – "legitimized" by the breadth of data and the technicality of the algorithms (which, remember, are mostly not publically available and opaque) – is said, in turn, to produce exact and, once again, neutral analyses that have the value of scientific truth, as will be discussed later. In addition to the fact that there is no such thing as a neutral technique, it should be remembered that Big Data is constituted by organizations which use it (and/or sell it to other organizations) with specific aims.

However, this wide-ranging ambition neglects three types of reduction of the real:

– Big Data stores the *representations* of the real (and not the real itself, a useful distinction to remember with regard to what is written on the topic) in the form of digitally coded data, digitization being by definition a reduction of the real;

– data only process what has already been digitized, which is just a tiny part of the real, even if we are only considering the life of human societies;

– not all digital data are collected and not all the possible types of processing are applied to it: the choice of data and processing depend on the organization's objectives which constitute Big Data (and finances the costs, which is very high).

It should be noted that an aspect that reinforces the *illusion of the real* is, once again, the complex intertwining between the global real and its part that only exists in and through digitization. Indeed, certain actions carried out by a person, such as making an online purchase, sending a message on a social network and looking for information on a search engine, are performed and can only be performed through the intermediary of digital tools linked to the Internet; furthermore, processing in real time the history of the tracks left by this individual modifies, in return, the interface of the sites used. There is a close relationship here between the representation of the real (the profile of this user, the code or the image of a product, the payment transaction, etc.) and the fraction of the real that is generated by and in digitization (the fact of being able to buy online, communicate via electronic messages, see a system's responses adapt to the actions we have completed in the past, etc.).

3.1.10. *DSS as systems of influence: persuasive technologies*

In addition to the structuring role of IS and DSS – which in part remain hidden – and recommendation systems – which want to suggest choices to a user whose free will is apparently not (or at least not totally) denied – new uses of digital information systems are emerging and making a name for themselves as *persuasive* technologies.

In the domain of DSS, Hosack [HOS 07] conducted a series of experiments based on two theories from psychology. *Operant conditioning* theory states that the consequences of a behavior will influence this behavior. *Reactance* theory shows that a person's behavior or beliefs can be negatively influenced by what they are ordered or suggested to do (the person, therefore, behaves in the opposite way than expected). Hosack demonstrates that feedback has a significant effect on decision-making behavior. He suggests using DSS interfaces to improve the compatibility of decisions made with the help of a DSS with the personal values of the decision makers and the values of the organization, as they have been entered into the system. In a successive study, Hosack and Paradice [HOS 14] suggest:

> (...) that practitioners and Information System (IS) researchers should consider user values when designing computerized decision feedback to adjust a system's design such that the potential user backlash is avoided or congruence between organizational and personal values is achieved.

Another example is the applied field of research at the intersection of psychology and IT known as *captology*. This term derives from the acronym CAPT (computers as persuasive technologies), but it is difficult not to link it to the verb *to capture*. The main creator of the concept of captology presents the questioning behind it [FOG 10]:

> How could you computerize persuasion? In other words, how could you use the power of computers to change what people believed, how they behaved, and how could this then be applied to improve the world in some way?

The website of the laboratory[11] defines captology as follows:

> Captology is the study of computers as persuasive technologies. This includes the design, research, and analysis of interactive computing products (computers, mobile phones, websites, wireless technologies, mobile

---

11 See captology.stanford.edu.

applications, video games, etc.) created for the purpose of changing people's attitudes or behaviors. BJ Fogg derived the term *captology* in 1996 from an acronym: Computers As Persuasive Technologies = CAPT.

Captology, therefore, involves designing digital systems (and particularly ambient systems[12]) with the absolutely explicit aim of modifying users' ways of thinking or behaving and, as such, the decisions they take.

The principle of influence techniques is not new: in the 1920s, Edward Bernays invented what he called "the engineering of consent"[13], as mentioned in Chapter 2. Captology ties in, in some way, with these origins and positions itself as a digital manipulation technique. It is worth pointing out that the examples given in the work conducted by the leading lab in this field of research, the Stanford Persuasive Tech Lab, are very "virtuous" and mostly concern applications intending to modify behaviors that put individuals' health at risk (smoking, unhealthy diets, lack of exercise, etc.).

However, we remain perplexed in the face of the absence of serious questioning about the free will of every individual and, simultaneously, the right we have to attempt to influence the behavior of a person in a way that is invisible and imperceptible to them.

This sort of questioning has, nevertheless, existed for a very long time, from the start of Athenian democracy in fact. Concerned about the power that rhetoric had on opinion, Aristotle encouraged all citizens to learn about it such that they would possess the same arms

---

12 Two authors, Kourouthanassis and Giaglis [KOU 06], describe ambient or ubiquitous computing as follows (our emphasis): "Instead of having IT in the foreground, triggered, manipulated, and used by humans, nowadays we witness that IT (irrespectively whether it comprises of computers, small sensors, or other communication means) gradually resides in the background, *monitoring the activities of humans*, processing and communicating this information to other sources and *intervening should it be required*".

13 Bernays' work influenced those in charge of Nazi propaganda (they used his public opinion manipulation techniques), but the author was also the originator of public relations and largely determined the development of advertising.

to defend their point of view. Likewise, Thucydides denounced the role of what we would now call "elements of language" (which he named perversion of language) in the outbreak of war[14].

It should be noted that opportunities to really influence individual decision-making are greatly increased by the detailed and evolutive image that we have of an individual through data generated by the ambient devices they use and the profile(s) attached to these (profiles generated by Big Data).

3.1.11. Conclusion

This section described a set of factors likely to influence the decision-making process and ultimately the decision made. Without denying the positive support DSS can bring to decision-making, in the next section we would like to emphasize the risks inherent to these tools and of which we ought to be aware such that they can be tackled as effectively as possible.

3.2. Risks linked to the use of DSS in decision-making

The first risk, from which the others derive, is the very pronounced imbalance between the different types of information a decision maker will process during the decision-making process. The omnipresence of IT systems in organizations' lives, the multiplication of devices with access to DSS (computers, mobiles, tablets, smart phones, etc.), which enable on the move and out of working hours access, the apparent low cost of this data for a given decision maker, the impression of time saving and the prestige associated with mastering these applications all lead to digital tools being favored as the only providers of information to accompany decision-making.

In this context, and due to the characteristics of the IT systems and DSS, as described above, there is the concern that decision makers do not develop a "made-to-measure" representation of the problem, but

---

14 Cited by [ATL 14].

rather use, often unconsciously, the "turnkey" representations included within these systems. Turnkey representations are by definition standard and provide a precise view of the world, the organization and its mission, and what is or is not "effective", etc. (via the "abstracts of the good").

3.2.1. *Inaccuracies in the results produced*

When there are errors in the results produced by the DSS, there is clearly the risk that wrong decisions will be made. The source of the errors can be:

– the data itself: during the collection of data and selection and integration processing in DSS;

– processing analyzing this data.

3.2.1.1. *Errors from data*

Quality (in the limited sense of accuracy) is a recurrent problem in IT systems as well as in their part concerning procedures (conventional IT systems) and their part dedicated to decision-making (DSS).

Errors can originate from the sources themselves, can involve the breakdown of devices sending the data (and which, therefore, stop providing data for a certain period of time) as well as *blind spots* in collection. Crawford [CRA 13a], citing a study [GRI 13] about the processing of flows of messages from social networks during Hurricane Sandy, comments:

> But these data don't represent the whole picture. The greatest number of tweets about Sandy came from Manhattan. This makes sense given the city's high level of smartphone ownership and Twitter use, but it creates the illusion that Manhattan was the hub of the disaster. Very few messages originated from more severely affected locations, such as Breezy Point, Coney Island and Rockaway. As extended power blackouts drained batteries and limited cellular access, even fewer tweets

came from the worst hit areas. In fact, there was much more going on outside the privileged, urban experience of Sandy that Twitter data failed to convey, especially in aggregate.

Crawford proposes the notion of *signal problems* which she defines as:

Data are assumed to accurately reflect the social world, but there are significant gaps, with little or no signal coming from particular communities.

Organizational problems can also generate inaccuracies in data. This is typically the case when a too restrictive rule, set in the IT system, is bypassed by employees who enter inaccurate data in the system to perform their task and meet objectives concerning deadlines, effectiveness, etc. A classic example is that of orders being placed with suppliers without following the official procedures, which should involve entering all the ordering information and waiting for the supplier's quote before confirmation. In an emergency situation, workers can place orders over the phone, the order can be accepted without official confirmation (on the basis of trust) and the information can be entered after the order has been placed and sometimes even after it has been received. The indicator measuring supplier performance by the time period between the placement of an order and its receipt is, therefore, distorted, as some such time periods are negative (the order is received before the order is placed according to the information entered).

Management by indicators, and its consequent feedback effect (see section 3.2.3.1), can also cause bypasses and the input of inaccurate data. A relatively recent example is a superior conducting an evaluation of his/her workers (an evaluation that had a direct impact on how a bonus package would be divided). In a large company (the name of which will not be provided), employees were evaluated according to three criteria, which gave three grades from which the application calculated the final grade. Faced with this system, the head of department was able to say (*sic*) "*I* know what I want the final grade to be, so I'll see to it that the 3 grades produce the result that I want". If this attitude is widespread across this company (which according to our information is very likely), then any data processing concerning not the final grade but the grades for each criterion will produce distorted results.

Some data errors remain undetected, whereas others are identified very (and even too) late. A famous example, which is also very memorable because of the millions of dollars that were lost as a consequence, is the Climate Orbiter probe which disintegrated before its intended landing on Mars in 1999. An investigation showed that two programs working together as the probe approached Mars did not use the same units – one used the imperial system, while the other used the metric system – and nobody noticed the error. The decision to slow down the probe's descent toward Mars could not be made in time as the distance "displayed" was still (though incorrectly) too great.

Big Data is often deemed to be indifferent toward data errors as they have an insignificant impact on results, given the considerable total volume of data. However, this overly optimistic view is denounced by several studies. Krasnow and Bruening [KRA 14] comment that:

> Big data proponents argue now that analytic tools are able to work on entire, massively large datasets, flaws in the underlying data do not significantly affect outcomes. They argue that [when] technology could only handle smaller data sizes, margin of error was an issue because samples rather than entire data sets were analyzed and results were extrapolated to describe the whole. But, practical experience shows that significant swaths of these faults can exist in the data and programmed tests for data quality can miss them. This results in matches not being identified, most often resulting in underrepresentation of one characteristic or group and overrepresentation of another.

3.2.1.2. *Processing errors*

Data errors naturally produce errors in the results, though often the totality of these errors is not perceived. Nevertheless, some errors are attributable to processing itself.

A now famous example is the Google Flu Trends application's estimation error in its predictions for the flu epidemic in the United States. In 2013, the forecasts (for the peak of the flu) overestimated the real figures by about 100% [LAZ 14]. Had public decisions been based exclusively on these data, they would have resulted in poorly targeted actions and an ineffective use of public funds. Fortunately, public officials did not rely blindly on these results to allocate health funds.

Other risks are related not to the data or processing but to the *way* in which they are both perceived by users of the DSS.

3.2.2. **Confusing the map and the territory**

As mentioned before, IS are systems that represent the real. A very common error of judgment consists of considering the representations of the real provided by DSS to be strictly identical or totally equivalent to the real itself. This type of error can be understood as confusing a map with the territory it represents.

This error can be an illusion of an exhaustive representation of a set (space, system, etc.) or an object (understood in the broad sense including people, concepts, etc.). In the case of the latter, the error concerns forgetting what has been lost in digitization, the uncoded part of the object or, beyond that, what is *irreducible* to coding.

3.2.2.1. *An illustration of an exhaustive representation of a set*

As shown above, data which are collected automatically come from digital sources, which, of course, do not constitute themselves the totality of the real. There can, therefore, be effects of distortion which, if not corrected by human interpretation and comparison with other sources, can represent a risk for decision-making. "Signal problems", the blind spots in data collection, as mentioned above, can lead decision makers to this type of error.

Crawford [CRA 13a] describes a smartphone application used by Boston city council to locate potholes in the town, StreetBump, so as to support the decision-making process of where to allocate resources to repair the roads. The data collected by the application presented blind spots, "signal problems": sectors of the population with lower incomes (particularly the elderly) have fewer smartphones than the wealthier sectors of the population (only 16% for elderly people in certain neighborhoods). Fortunately, officials of the City of Boston did not fall for the illusion that StreetBump presented an exhaustive representation of the state of the roads and, therefore, worked with researchers to complete the data so as to avoid only repairing the roads used by smartphone users.

3.2.2.2. Forgetting what is lost in digitization

We can consider that everything has the potential to be digitally coded, if we are willing to pay the "price" of reduced complexity. Affective computing codes emotions and feelings. Questions, however, should be asked about the part of the real that is lost in coding. What has been lost between the digital data, which represents a feeling of empathy in an IT application, and the emotional experience that a person can have of this feeling throughout their life and in their relationships with other humans?[15]

In the case of a merger between two enterprises, can decisions regarding the distribution of employees into teams or services be effectively made based on the information available in the IT system alone? Can the sum of these data enable an evaluation of workers' (positive or negative) contribution toward the collective work, the type of role they play in a crisis situation, their capacity to engage in a new entity, their contribution to a positive evolution of the enterprise, etc., which are skills decisive for the longevity of the new entity.

---

15 Poet Robert Frost once said: "Poetry is what gets lost in translation". Yet, he was talking about translation between two (human) languages which are, however, much more expressive than digital coding.

3.2.3. *The risk of losing diversity*

Another type of risk affecting the quality of decisions concerns the feedback effects produced by the use of an IT system due to its performative nature.

The so-called subprime mortgage crisis is an illustration of a massive effect of feedback to decisions made using tools to support the financial management of market evolution, as observed by Abrams [ABR 14]:

> Models used in the mortgage securitization market to assign risk to sub-prime mortgages in the first decade of this century are examples of data scientists not understanding how the models themselves would influence the behavior of various market players. That change in behavior affected the model validity helping to facilitate a market decline.

3.2.3.1. *The vicious circle of feedback*

Countless examples exist where the performative effects of classifications and indicators produce feedback effects.

The classification of medical treatments, which correspond to tariffs to be reimbursed by health insurance, has resulted in some health services overprescribing costly procedures and neglecting activities with a lower cost.

Indicators are the cause of multiple feedbacks. In these cases, the activity is no longer oriented toward achieving objectives but toward (only) improving corresponding indicators, which may, in the end, be contrary to the global objectives of the organization.

A notion linked to the feedback effect is that of perverse incentive, where (material or symbolic) rewards, aimed at improving the organization's results, have the exact opposite effect. A very famous and delightful example of perverse incentive is that of the French authorities in Indochina. To reduce the rat population, the French authorities decided to give an award for every dead rat that was brought to them. In response, the Indochinese started breeding rats.

In organizations, these rewards are attributed on the basis of performance indicators. Some call centers, which considered the number of calls received by a worker to be an acceptable indicator of their performance, experienced employees hanging up during the call to be able to accept more calls. In an enterprise, the decision to give a reward to sales assistants based on the turnover they make encourages them to focus on selling products with a low margin.

One of the most popular decision support tools, dashboards, which combine sets of indicators, may well lead to decisions that have a different and sometimes opposite effect to that intended. The ease of obtaining dashboards must not exempt managers from collecting additional information to evaluate the situation before making a decision. The risk is, in fact, that decision makers will look for information where it is simplest to find, i.e. in the many charts and reports provided by the DSS. In so doing, decision makers find themselves in the situation of the drunkard from the joke who, one night, was found looking for his keys under a streetlamp (although they were lost in the darkness) because "this is where the light is".

3.2.3.2. *IS representing a unique worldview*

As mentioned before, views of the same "object" can differ and, beyond that, even the existence of an object can be perceived differently. Yet, in the overwhelming majority of cases, IS and IT systems only reflect *one* worldview, which organizes the set of the data they store or produce. By the feedback effect, this unique view is reinforced by the use of IT systems, even when the view is not necessarily what will enable the organization to be as efficient as possible, especially in the long term.

An example, in the life of territorial authorities, is the different views of what constitutes a territory. It should be noted that territories are an essential "object" for decision-making concerning the economic development of a region. IS used by the regions correspond to a representation of the territory that most often relates to administrative division, which may match the National Statistics Institute's economic zones (employment zone, urban zone, rural zone, etc.). This representation considers the territory to be static, postulated, a space *demarcated by borders*, and equipped with a finite amount of resources. However, at least one other representation of the territory exists, which views it as a dynamic process of *concentrating actors into inter-relationships*. In the case of the latter, the territory is *revealed* over the course of the process and its resources cannot be accessed outside this process [COL 93]. The concepts considered are not the same for the two cases. A region's policy may, for example, focus on competitivity, which presupposes a densification of the industrial base and industry–research relationships, relating therefore to the second view of the territory. However, here as elsewhere, "stewardship is in charge" and an IS centered on a static representation of the territory will necessarily result in an implementation of policies according to a static view of a territory, as region officials will be guided and constrained by a set of tools (data capture, information collecting from National Statistics Institute, index and indicator calculations, dashboard constitution, benchmarking with other regions, etc.). These tools are all offshoots of the first view of the territory and contradict the view that is necessary if the announced policy is to be effectively applied, and which, in the end, cannot be implemented [SAL 13a, SAL 07b].

We must, therefore, not be deceived, in an organization, by the abundance of technical tools for IT systems; these tools are most often centered on one worldview, which is generally not made explicit and is endlessly replicated.

The danger is, in the spirit of the joke attributed to Paul Watzlawick[16], *that decision support tools only offer decision makers a hammer and thus lead them look at all problems as if they were nails.*

The main risk here is the loss of diversity, which would have effects that are at best limiting, at worst destructive to the

---

16... but also, in slightly different forms, to Abraham Maslow, Bill Gates and a number of others: "If your only tool is a hammer, every problem looks like a nail".

organization's ability to innovate. Innovation is in fact only possible if the enterprise has the ability to generate *innovative representations* (with regard to its skills, markets, products, economic environment, etc.). It is worth remembering that innovation is nowadays considered to be the primary factor of the competitiveness of enterprises [MOA 08]. The situation is very similar for public institutions. To ensure sustainable economic development, a territorial authority must implement innovative representations of what constitutes a territory, a resource, an economic player, an industrial sector, etc.

We will return to the attention that should be paid to the worldviews inscribed in IS, and particularly in IT systems and DSS, in Chapter 4.

This loss of diversity may be further aggravated by the widespread use of predictive tools linked to Big Data.

3.2.4. *Toward more and more predictivity?*

Decision support has always proposed systems that enable a future situation to be forecast with varying degrees of effectiveness. However, for Big Data, this ability to predict is its primary purpose and is constantly stressed by its promoters.

3.2.4.1. *Risk loathing*

In addition to the aforementioned problems of inaccurate predictions, a danger here is an aggravated reduction of diversity by massive effects of feedback. Models predicting consumer behavior will, therefore, favor the most purchased products, perhaps to the detriment of products that may be more suited to the real needs (rather than the inferred needs) of the consumer.

A recent article[17] regarding predictive recruitment is concerned about future "clone factories". The paper also mentions the possibility of errors being made in recruitment, given that desired profiles are defined from Big Data and standard needs of enterprises, and do not

---

17 See www.parlonsrh.com/vous-avez-dit-recrutement-predictif/, 15 October 2014.

necessarily correspond to the needs of a particular enterprise, in a specific situation, with its own project.

A number of voices have been raised to draw attention to the risk of aggravating social inequalities through the use of Big Data. With regard to health, Krasnow and Waterman [KRA 14] remark:

> Similarly, analytics used with big data related to health care (…) may raise serious concerns for individuals when that same analysis is used to assess his or her eligibility for health insurance coverage or for certain medical treatments.

and Crawford [CRA 13a] questions:

> As we move into an era in which personal devices are seen as proxies for public needs, we run the risk that already existing inequities will be further entrenched. Thus, with every big data set, we need to ask which people are excluded. Which places are less visible? What happens if you live in the shadow of big data sets?

Remember, for promoters of Big Data, data errors are not significant due to the large volumes that are processed. Therefore, and although Big Data designers are called *data scientists*, an in-depth understanding of the *data*, of what measures (or does not measure) a source, distortions introduced by this or that source (all of which are subjects well understood by field sociologists), does not seem to be a concern for the sector.

More generally, we can be concerned about the risk loathing that comes with the passion for predictivity served by Big Data. Once again, the brakes may be applied to innovation, which inherently includes an element of risk (higher the newer the innovation).

3.2.4.2. *From predictive to prescriptive*

Finally, the generalization of predictive processing can promote the principle of results which could not be questioned (due to the volumes of data, the sophistication of the algorithms and the anathema placed on looking for causation) and which would, therefore, reach a *prescriptive* status, which is already supported by the most fervent proselytes of Big Data [MAY 13].

Prescriptive results may finally open the door to automated decision-making, causing multiple problems, at the legal and moral levels (who will take the final responsibility for the decision?), as well as in the case of public institutions, at the level of democracy.

Faced with this type of risk, it is necessary to take a look at the types of reasoning at work in the predictive processing of Big Data, which causes obvious epistemological problems.

3.2.4.3. *Epistemological problems*

The discourses of Big Data promoters operate a number of epistemological shifts. There follows several examples.

3.2.4.3.1. Flattening the logical levels: macro = Σ micro?

The difference between the micro level and the macro level is assimilated to a difference in *volume* rather than in *nature*. The macro level is confused with the sum of the elements of the micro level: society is the sum of individuals it comprises, the economy is the sum of enterprises, a person is the sum of their consumer preferences or digital tracks, etc.

This naturally results in concepts, reasoning or laws specific to the micro level being applied to the macro level as a matter of course. It should be noted that this is the case when the same indicator – which is simply increasingly aggregated – is used to support decisions at increasingly higher levels.

3.2.4.3.2. Is correlation really better than causation?

This second example concerns a sometimes violent contesting [AND 08, MAY 13] of looking for causation, which is the basis of the scientific approach. The interest of causation is fiercely denied as it will soon be (advantageously) replaced by correlation. However, though looking for correlations can be used to establish causation, it cannot be seen as capable of replacing it, in terms of scientific reasoning or in data processing for decision support. An example of confusing correlation with causation is a study that established a causal link between the consumption of chocolate in one country and the number of Nobel prizes it was awarded [MES 12], when in fact it was only a case of (strong) correlation, i.e. two variables that evolved in the same way (without being able to claim that one caused the other). The study received a great deal of ridicule and prompted new absurd correlations to be found, such as the consumption of chocolate and the number of serial killers or the number of road accidents and the number of Nobel prizes awarded.[18]

In the French reference newspaper *Le Monde*, an article of two researchers on genetics [PRU 14] reminds researchers of the need to *test* hypotheses (which correlations identified in Big Data can help to produce):

> However the question must be asked: do Big Data and the correlations it produces have demonstration values? Can they replace the experimental approach and disregard causality tests? The two approaches are not exclusive, but rather complementary. Large scale approaches are a precious tool for exploring complex biological phenomena and revealing unexpected relationships between variables. These correlations must, however, be considered as hypotheses to be tested. To date, nothing replaces the strength of experimental tests and Cartesian analysis to identify links of causality. Though the need for this experimental step is sometimes called into question as it is long and expensive, it remains no less of an essential pillar of understanding.

This can also be applied to decision-making, which must be based on data from varied sources and on-the-ground knowledge, on experience. Stiegler [STI 14], using Kant, identifies an illuminating distinction:

---

18 See replicatedtypo.com/wp-content/uploads/2012/11/ChocolateSerialKillers_Winters Roberts.pdf.

"(…) Kant poses the problem of the relationship between calculation and interpretation such that he draws a distinction between understanding and reason:

– understanding is *analytical*, i.e. it can be transformed into calculation (calculator or big data), it can be *automated*;

– but *reason* is not understanding, it is what collects the data captured from experience or intuition in order to *judge*, to make *decisions* (this is the experience of the reign of end purposes)".

3.2.4.3.3. Data = information = knowledge?

A final example, which goes beyond Big Data and concerns IS in general, is the commonly made assimilation of three very distinct concepts: data, information and knowledge. Let us go over a number of definitions of these terms.

Data is the "records or descriptions or memories of events or objects" for Bateson [BAT 72], who agrees with Mélèse's [MÉL 79] more precise description of "the recording in an agreed code of the measurement of certain attributes of an object or an event". Data itself does not have a meaning. For instance, "the revenue of company X was 30 million euros in 2014" is data.

Information is the data that has been contextualized, interpreted and that has meaning. Bateson's [BAT 72] famous definition of information as "any difference which makes a difference in some later event" has inspired other authors such as Davenport and Prusak [DAV 98], who describe information as "data that makes a difference", a message that "changes the way the recipient perceives something". According to Mélèse [MÉL 79], "for a human being (or an automaton) any signal, message or perception that has an impact on their behavior or cognitive state is information". To transform the previous example into information, the data must be contextualized: "revenue is 30 million euros, in 2013 it was 35 million euros and in

2012 it was 37 million euros; the average revenue of enterprises in the sector has progressed over the same period, etc.".

Knowledge is based on information and cannot be dissociated from experience, as the citation attributed to Albert Einstein states: "the only source of knowledge is experience, everything else is just information". Davenport and Prusak [DAV 98] describe knowledge as:

> Knowledge is a fluid mix of framed experience, values, contextual information, and expert insight that provides a framework for evaluating and incorporating new experiences and information. It originates and is applied in the minds of knowers.

Knowledge requires a *subject* (i.e. a human). Knowledge arises from experience and enables action, which is not the case for information (nor *a fortiori* for data). As Paulré [PAU 01] wrote: "knowledge is an organization of representation in that it enables the organization of action (external or internalized in thought)". In the example described above, knowledge is what enables enterprise leaders to make a decision or a series of decisions: to launch a study on clients, to rework the pricing system, to restrict products ranges, to abandon an activity, etc. This knowledge is composed of their experience in the enterprise and in other enterprises, their competencies, their intuition, their view of the mission of the enterprise, etc. Knowledge cannot, therefore, be attained: only, its *expressions* can be studied or managed, mostly through actions and language.

Though data, information and knowledge involve relationships, they are actually not of the same nature and confusing them causes an (additional) epistemological problem. This also questions the place that could be given to DSS (which process data and produce information, and not knowledge) if the trend accelerated by Big Data comes true, a place that could then be called usurpatory. As Paulré [PAU 01] reminds readers:

Knowledge and information are relational in nature. Data only becomes information through the effect it is likely to produce on behavior. Nevertheless, it should be stressed that a procedure, plan or representation can be schematized, modeled and coded and thereby lose this relational character. However, it must be noted, that in so doing, they change in nature. They can in fact move not as knowledge, but as data. They are only knowledge in so far as they can be correctly interpreted and used. So-called "coded" knowledge is only really knowledge in that it can be assimilated and used by a subject to reorganize or complete previous knowledge.

3.2.4.3.4. Conclusion

The flattening of the logical levels, looking for causation's regression toward looking for simple correlations, assimilating knowledge and data, all paint a general picture: the refusal of the irreductible diversity of the real, the denial of the necessary complexity of human thought and the devaluation of experience as the primary source of knowledge.

3.2.5. *Exacerbated risks in the case of decisions defining the management system*

It should be noted that all the aforementioned risks are much higher when decisions that are "under influence" regard the definition of the management system and not "only" the concrete implementation of action (see Chapter 1, section 1.3.5). Remember that the decisions defining the management system will set the framework within which action decisions will be made. Indeed, decisions defining the management system concern identifying objectives, constraints and resources, defining methods (management, work and project management), developing indicators, etc.

The high-level representations that the organization produces about itself (what is its mission, what are its values, etc.), about its environment (what is its range in the space and in terms of activities, what is its evolution, etc.) and about the relationships it has with the environment (are they directed toward competition and/or cooperation, do these relationships involve the moral responsibility of the organization, etc.) have a profound influence on the organization of the management system.

In the case of decisions defining the management system, it is now more essential than ever that the option for different worldviews be maintained and that the views implemented in DSS are made *explicit* such that they can, if need be, be questioned.

Conclusion: key points for DSS design

The most serious errors are due to the definition of the problem

The decision process can be assimilated to the problem-solving process. In the first step of the process, the problem is formulated and structured. This determines, to a large extent, the final decision. This is in line with the central importance of the *intelligence* phase in Simon's model.

During this phase, so-called type III errors concern the definition of the problem itself. They can result in the wrong problem being solved precisely. In DSS, the authority of the results produced using sophisticated systems can effectively help mask this type of error, the consequences of which can be dramatic. It is, therefore, worth paying a great deal of attention to the way in which the problem is formulated.

Mental representations play a key role in defining the problem

Mental representations, in the broad sense of world views, value systems, perspectives, etc., are decisive to the way in which a problem is identified and then defined. These representations are the representations of the decision maker, of the organization of which they are part and, more generally, of the society in which it exists.

IS, IT systems and DSS bring "turnkey" representations

IS are in essence systems of representation(s) that drastically reduce the "real". Due to the characteristics of digital technology, this reduction is further accentuated in their IT and DSS components. Both of the latter contain, in the majority of cases invisibly, world views that are imposed on their users and which become the one obligatory framework (the only accessible reality) in which they perform their task or build the definition of the problem. The interactive and adaptive character of IT systems and DSS can lead users to change their behavior, which is sometimes deliberately sought by these systems.

DSS design must be accompanied by a reflection on the influence they can have.

The risk of confusing the "real" and its coding

Predetermining the understanding of situations generated by IS and strangely DSS, itself involves a number of risks. Out of these, a major risk is confusing the real and its coding. Considering what is represented in a DSS to be the only foundation can lead to only the part of the "real" that has been coded (which is by definition not exhaustive) to be taken into account, and therefore to mistakenly neglect new elements which have not yet been coded or are uncodable. It is noted that these uncoded or uncodable elements could be perceived and processed through consultations with human players internal or external to the enterprise.

The loss of diversity: a major risk for maintaining innovation skills

The reduction of the real by the IS (including DSS), if it is not questioned and compensated for, can lead to a loss of diversity, particularly in decision-making. The effect is all the greater with regard to unstructured decisions or undefined problems, for which the representation of the problem totally determines the decision made. These decisions are primarily decisions defining the management system, as well as all decisions related to innovation. Relating to all dimensions of the organization, innovation inherently requires innovative views of the organization, its activities, its environment, etc.

The risks of looking uncontrollably for prediction

Big Data and its uses, as planned by their promoters, involve an additional number of risks. Big Data is said to be able to, more than other systems, produce predictable results. Yet, processed data, on the one hand, only consider digital sources and, on the other hand, contain "blind spots". It is easy to understand the risk of these decisions, which would blindly follow the systems' predictions, decisions which due to their performative effect would produce a *self-fulfilling prophecy*, reinforcing or even creating the simplified view produced by Big Data in the real.

The responsibility of DSS designers and other stakeholders

Faced with these risks, on the one hand, and the major issues facing organizations and societies (economic and social, environmental, cultural and societal), on the other hand, DSS designers have a real *responsibility*: which perspective(s), which concepts and which freedom of choice will they include (or not include) in the DSS? By proposing a set of concepts related to a unique worldview (which is not generally explicit) in the DSS, the designer runs the risk of limiting the ability to innovate in decision-making, of guiding the decision toward one determined direction (which, for instance, would represent the interests of one sole stakeholder) or even of making it impossible to implement a strategy. Chapter 4 will discuss the responsibility of the players in DSS design.

Elements for Ethical DSS Design

Introduction: being responsible for one's actions and ethical requirements

One of the key roles of information systems (IS), and especially decision support systems (DSS), must be to help build innovative representations or, at least, to not hinder their production by coding a unique view of the organization and its environment, thus having the power of law [SAL 13a].

Designers of DSS, therefore, have a major responsibility. But it must not be forgotten that these systems are produced by and for organizations, are financed by the latter (sometimes very heavily, like in the case of Big Data), are designed, developed and maintained by engineers and technicians, and are used by employees and the organization's other partners. Therefore, a whole set of players shares a responsibility for DSS design. This responsibility is *economical* in the sense that it must support the creation of representations capable of guaranteeing the development of the organization. It is also *social* due to the consequences that low innovation can have at the level of the organization and even beyond. By "responsibility", we mean moral responsibility (and not merely accountability), i.e. a person must hold their actions up to their conscience, their *ethical* values[1].

---

1 This chapter is in part inspired by [SAL 15].

Section 4.1 will focus on a brief state of the art of computer ethics. The field can be seen as still being in the definition phase, although it was born at the same time as computing (called cybernetics at the time). With research conducted by philosophers and computer scientists, computer ethics has strangely been neglected by the latter both at the level of research and teaching. Computer ethics is part of the thousand-year tradition of reflecting about ethics in general; an overview will be provided via the presentation of a number of broad ethical theories (concerning the individual as well as the enterprise). The remainder of the section will focus on the themes of computer ethics and on a number of its theories. The ethical values supported, in addition to approaches integrating ethical values in DSS development, will then be presented.

DSS-specific computer ethics will be the focus of section 4.2. Although research in the domain of DSS barely touches on the question, it is, from a brief state of the art, possible to identify two approaches, which are based on whether the ethics focus on the decisions made or on the decision process itself. It will be noted that Big Data – due to its lack of respect for the private life of individuals – has prompted a certain interest in ethics and resulted in specific ethical approaches. The issues related to DSS will then be noted, particularly, the need to maintain as far as possible organizations' ability to innovate. Choosing the ethical value of *democracy* will then be proposed, as we believe it is the value most capable of implementing the need for the DSS to have a diversity of views inscribed in it. Nevertheless, calling on the responsibility of DSS designers, upon which we insisted above, is only legitimate when this responsibility is assisted and equipped, i.e. made the object of an *engineering of responsibility*.

Section 4.3 is a contribution to this type of engineering, which will here focus on the early requirements analysis phase. The methodological tool we will propose is a three-level model, which can reveal how a doxa, a general view of an entity (i.e. an object, like the enterprise, or a category, like work), and the ethical values accompanying it, is progressively embodied in structuring principles and then in restrictive standards (concrete expression of the ethical values or absence thereof). For illustrative purposes, the methodological tool is applied to the category of *evaluation* to analyze how the value of *democracy* can be respected or, conversely, prevented. Two evaluation doxai will be explored: the first currently dominating and the second representing a possible alternative.

4.1. Computer ethics

4.1.1. *A brief history*

Ethical concerns have been expressed since the dawn of computing in the work of Norbert Wiener. From 1948, he perceived the potentially considerable effects at the social level of what he called *cybernetics*:

> Long before Nagasaki and the public awareness of the atomic bomb, it had occurred to me that we were here in the presence of another social potentiality of unheard-of importance for good and for evil.

Norbert Wiener then adopts a very political position. Alarmed by the possible use of cybernetics as a tool for control by certain groups ("Fascists, Strong Men in Business, and Government"), he devotes his book *The Human Use of Human Beings: Cybernetics and Society* (1989, orig. 1950) "to a protest against this inhuman use of human beings".

In the 1970s, Mowshowitz and Weizenbaum would also adopt a critical stance against the possible social impacts of computing. Mowshowitz [MOW 76] considers that:

> Most computer-based information processing systems [...] are seen to serve one of two general social functions: the coordination of diversity or the control of disorder. Coordination and control signify the extremes of a continuum of social choices.

He supports the need to organize vigilance to avoid a shift toward the "control" pole of this continuum. For his part, Weizenbaum

[WEI 76] endeavored to define the domains in which computing applications should never be used:

> The point is […] that there are some human functions for which computers *ought* not to be substituted. It has nothing to do with what computers can or cannot be made to do. Respect, understanding, and love are not technical problems.

He proposes installing an impassable ethical border between human beings and computer systems and, moreover, excluding from computing all human functions that involve interpersonal relations.

Since the 1980s, computer ethics has constituted a field of research in its own right. It has become pluridisciplinary, welcoming in particular researchers from the domain of philosophy [MOO 85, JOH 85, BYN 85]. The effect of philosophy would be felt for a long time on computer ethics; to information technology (IT) system specialists, its theories can appear abstract, even abstruse, and difficult to apply to practice.

In the 1990s, a new branch of computer ethics emerged: professional ethics. Professional ethics appeals for ethics to be included in training courses for developers and in the methods for developing IT systems [GOT 91, WAL 93].

Over the past 15 years, the Internet, its uses, the wide-ranging control capacities it offers, etc., have characterized debates held by specialists in computer ethics and within the general public of users, centering on reflections about the rights of individuals (to confidentiality, to access information, etc.) and their duties (see the notion of *netiquette*).

Although they are widely recognized, ethical questions are still for the most part dealt with *outside* the domain of IT systems and remain marginal in mainstream publications, as Mingers and Walsham noted [MIN 10]:

Despite the massive effects that developments in ICT are having on the world society, there has not been a huge literature on ethics within the mainstream of information systems journals.

Indeed, the tiny extent to which ethics has been dealt with in research about IT systems is striking. By way of example, in one of the most important journals in the domain, *MIS Quarterly*, only 14 articles have used the terms *ethics* or *responsibility* in their title, three of which were published in the past decade. The same is true in *Decision Support Systems*, a very representative journal in the domain of DSS, with only seven articles, five of which were published in the past 10 years.

Moreover, in many countries, ethics is broadly absent from IT courses and, when it does appear, it is most often reduced to a presentation of the rules set out by the administrative bodies that operate in accordance with the data protection legislation (like the CNIL in France)[2], which is the degree zero of ethics.

This lack of interest must be analyzed. One of its causes, in our opinion, is the problem of where computing should be positioned. In a confusion of technology and science, computing has been called a science (computer science) although there has never been an epistemological reflection on its object(s), methods, history and relationships with other sciences. Furthermore, the domain of IT has close links with the market: advances in academic research can, therefore, very quickly lead to technical products being sold by private companies. This certainly does not encourage specialists to reflect on the nature of the IT and its impact on society.

4.1.2. *Ethical theories*

Countless texts from the literature in computer ethics (which mostly, remember, do not come from the domain of IT systems) stress

---

2 Commission Nationale de l'Informatique et des Libertés (National Commission for Computing and Liberties).

the need to place research in terms of the large ethical theories. These theories concern the individual or the organization as a whole (particularly enterprises).

4.1.2.1. *Ethics at the level of the individual*

In the field of personal ethics, the two most frequently cited (and opposing) theories are consequentialism and Kantian ethics. Aristotelian ethics also appear, though less frequently.

For consequentialism (in particular, Bentham and Mill's utilitarism), only the consequences of an action can enable its ethical character to be judged. The moral imperative is to act by looking for the greatest good for the greatest number of people.

In Kantian ethics, the consequences of an action do not enable its moral value to be evaluated. It is an ethics of duty (deontology in the philosophical sense). The criterion of the moral action is that it can be made universal, which is expressed in the *categorical imperative* ([KAN 95], cited by [RIC 98]): "act only according to that maxim by which you can at the same time that it should become a universal law"; completed by a second imperative "so act as to treat humanity, whether in your own person or in another, always as an end, and never as only a means".

For Aristotle [ARI 14], living a *good life* is the aim of life. Ethics can be assimilated to looking for happiness (*eudaimonia*), which can only be attained by developing virtues. Moral actions, therefore, better individuals and by using their virtues (in particular, the ability to choose the happy medium, *phronesis*), they will be able to tell moral actions apart from immoral actions.

Remember that there are multiple ethical theories, which have brought about countless debates for nearly three millennia.

As stated above, researchers and professionals in IT often feel detached from these theories [CIG 13]. Stahl [STA 08a], who is a philosopher, comments that researchers in IT systems, faced with the complexity of ethical debates, are tempted to ignore philosophical theories and to work from a "common sense concept of ethics, where behaviors or views are accepted as ethical if respondents perceive them as ethical" and he concludes that "such an approach is not tenable".

Similarly, we can highlight the effort philosophers themselves must make such that their concepts can be used by researchers and practitioners in IT. Some philosophers are aware of this, such as Nissenbaum [NIS 98], who when writing about values such as justice, responsibility and autonomy commented:

> Out of these conceptions, in order to be able to map values to characteristics of computer systems, I must construct concepts that are operational within a practical setting, create precision where none naturally exists.

4.1.2.2. Ethics at the level of the enterprise

Ethics of the enterprise (considered as an entity) is dealt with in business ethics, which inspired the notion of the social responsibility of the enterprise [BOL 08]. Business ethics has given rise to a number theories that [SMI 99] describe as normative.

A first approach is stockholder theory, which holds that the enterprise's sole mission is to make profit, particularly to pay stockholders. The enterprise's moral behavior is inscribed within this mission and it is the managers and employees duty to act with the aim of maximizing profit, within the confines of the law, of course. The most well-known representative of this theory is Friedman, who titled one of his articles "The Social Responsibility of Business is to Increase its Profit" [FRI 70]. Stockholder theory pertains to the utilitarism as the consequences of actions will determine whether they are ethical or not (i.e. if they enable profit to be increased or not).

Stakeholder theory is the second main approach in business ethics. Although for some branches of the theory the list of stakeholders can be extensive, and include society as a whole, the stakeholders usually considered are either those *vital* to the success of the enterprise or those *vitally* affected by it [SMI 99]: stockholders, employees, suppliers, clients, local inhabitants and powers in the enterprise's area of activity, etc. Kantian ethics are applied here in the sense that stakeholders must not be considered to be merely a *means* by the senior management of the enterprise, but rather they must be respected as an *end*.

4.1.2.3. *The extent of human responsibility*

The concept of ethics, like the concept of responsibility, has evolved over time, particularly after the realization that human activity could put nature itself in danger. Jonas [JON 79] sets out a number of distinctive signs of what he calls *anthropocentric ethics* (to which the aforementioned theories belong). One such sign is the rapport of human activities that remains neutral toward the non-human world. Anthropocentric ethics, therefore, relates to a time when technology did not affect "the nature of things". The modern period, characterized by technology that has become "the most important enterprise of the species" sees the "triumph of *homo faber* over his external object". Jonas appeals to an ethics that recognizes the responsibility of mankind not only toward its contemporaries but also toward nature as a whole and future generations.

The position that we will support later in this chapter is inscribed, very modestly and of course in a limited way, to this great perspective.

4.1.3. *The values of computer ethics*

Some authors limit the list of values of computer ethics to four [MAS 86], known as the acronym PAPA: *privacy* (respecting private life), *accuracy* (the precision and reliability of information), *property* (respecting property) and *accessibility* (guaranteeing access to information). Nevertheless, in recent years, new values have been frequently cited, such as justice (which covers the concepts of fairness and non-discrimination), freedom (of speech and access to information), the autonomy of the user, freedom from bias, transparency, trust, informed consent, accountability (which establishes a link between an action or information and its author), universal usability, human welfare and democracy [FRI 02, BRE 10, FLO 10].

Values which are less often attached to the notion of ethics are sometimes added to this list, such as politeness, calmness and identity. Sustainable development is also seen to be an ethical value and even often represents the only context in which computer ethics is dealt with by a professional organization. The concept of neutrality, linked to the concept of bias, is generally used to refer to the risk that certain groups will be harmed by the IT system (for example, by the principle of categorization of query results or by an unequal representation of different groups). But it is also used in relation to the notion of *truth,* i.e. it is not ethical to shorten, mask or distort.

It should be noted that when *responsibility* is mentioned, very rarely does it concern social responsibility and it practically never concerns economical responsibility. Responsibility is generally linked to the notion of accountability. However, accountability is relatively limited and is principally oriented toward uncivil or fraudulent uses, when it is desirable to find out who has committed the crime.

With regard to the list of these values, Stahl [STA 08a, STA 08b] states that a great deal of research into computer ethics is located at the micro level and considers that the macro level is *given.* For the author, the macro level is the ontological level, that is where we specify how a certain number of essential entities are considered. It corresponds to what, in Chapter 3, we called *representations* or *worldviews.* At the macro level, the vision to be adopted for mankind could, for instance, be questioned: a human seeking to maximize their individual profit, or conversely, a human looking for social harmony. Likewise, the vision for an enterprise could be questioned: an entity whose *raison d'être* is to maximize profit for stockholders, or an institution which must produce goods or services useful for society (profit is, therefore, an objective and not a *raison d'être*). We will return to this topic in section 4.3 and propose a methodological tool to make these macro level views explicit.

4.1.4. *Ethics in IT system development*

4.1.4.1. *Types of uses considered*

A great deal of research is devoted to the *personal* (rather than professional) use of computers, and in particular applications available via the Internet. When *professional* uses are mentioned, it is usually in a very global and non-discriminatory way. The ethical values considered, therefore, do not differ from one type of use to another: the private life of employees must be respected, there must be no discrimination between groups of employees, employees must not send insulting e-mails to their colleagues, etc. A few authors have tackled the social consequences of IT systems, particularly about the nature of the work [STA 10].

It should be noted that within professional uses, the distinction between the use of IT to support the realization of a task and its use as decision support has not really been established by computer ethics.

4.1.4.2. *The development of IT systems*

As mentioned before, there is a certain distance (and even a gulf) between the work of researchers in computer ethics originally from humanities or social sciences and the practices of researchers and professionals in computing. This question has been brought up recurrently by both parties [ROG 00, NIS 98, BEL 04]. Van Den Hoven [VAN 08] therefore advocates "a proactive integration of ethics [...] in design, architecture, requirements, specifications, standards, protocols, incentive structures, and institutional arrangements".

For the past 15 years, a branch of research has focused on the *applicability* of computer ethics in the context of system development. A number of approaches have been proposed, including an ethical perspective in IT system design. The majority of these approaches have come from researchers in humanities or social sciences, often in cooperation with researchers in IT systems. They vary in terms of their level of exhaustivity, their degree of operationality and the number of their cases of application.

Some of these approaches seek to accompany as far as possible the organization of exchanges and negotiations between the different stakeholders. Mingers and Walsham [MIN 10] therefore propose using Habermas' discourse ethics [HAB 99] (1992, cited by the authors) to give the different stakeholders equal rights and reach consensus in the best possible conditions. Mingers and Walsham suggest that engineering methods of SSM-type[3] such as JAD[4] can be used in this approach.

Value sensitive design (VSD) is one of the most accomplished methods with regard to the inclusion of ethical dimensions in IT system development [FRI 02]. At the origin of VSD is the concept of *embedded values* in IT systems [NIS 98]. These values are encoded in systems, although system designers are not always aware of it. They are invisible, but nevertheless drive the operation of the IT system and may contradict the ethical values of the users. Cookies are one such example. Cookies enable sites to collect information about a connected person, without the person being aware of it, nor, *a fortiori*, having given their consent. This stands in contrast with the ethical value of informed consent.

VSD is an iterative methodology that includes three types of analysis: conceptual, empirical and technical.

Conceptual analysis primarily seeks to determine which stakeholders are directly or indirectly impacted by the system being developed and the way in which they are impacted. The values involved are then identified in order to build precise definitions for these values.

Empirical analysis studies the human and social, the individual and organizational context in which the system must function.

The final analysis, *technical* analysis, on the one hand seeks to evaluate whether the technical solutions envisioned would be a support or, conversely, an obstacle to taking stock of the values

---

3 Soft systems methodologies.
4 Joint application design.

retained and, on the other hand, proposes specific developments to support a particular value.

One of many pieces of software developed by integrating the VSD approach is UrbanSim [BOR 08]. UrbanSim is a DSS that helps plan a territory and is aimed at a broad set of stakeholders (local representatives, inhabitants, planners, etc.), enabling them to see the results of different evolution scenarios. The moral values supported by UrbanSim are justice (no discrimination against a group of stakeholders), accountability (stakeholders must be capable of checking that their values have been correctly translated into the system) and democracy (the system supports democratic debate).

In the perspective of VSD, Brey [BRE 10] introduces a distinction between two standard practices for the development, management and use of IT systems. Morally *transparent* practices are those that relate (positively or negatively) to obvious ethical values. *Opaque* practices are those which are not well known beyond a limited circle of specialists and have an impact on moral values, or known practices, but about which it is difficult to understand that they carry an ethical load. Brey proposes an approach that he calls *disclosive computer ethics*, which focuses on identifying practices that are morally opaque.

Some research seeks to bring the concepts of VSD closer to the concepts of requirements engineering so as to include as upstream as possible the requirement of respecting ethical values [DET 14].

4.2. Ethics in DSS development

4.2.1. *A brief history/state-of-the-art*

Though ethics in decision-making has been the subject of an abundance of literature in medicine and in the domain of management sciences, particularly for consultancy activities [COT 00], ethics in DSS remains a relatively unexplored domain.

Having found only an extremely limited number of articles about the topic of ethics in two major journals in the domain of decision support (*Decision Support Systems* and *Decision Sciences*), Meredith and Arnott [MER 03] express their disappointment:

> This paucity of published research and debate on the ethics of decision support in two of the discipline's premier journal is disappointing.

They also comment that:

> Given the popularity of data warehouse, business intelligence and other decision support systems, it is unfortunate that the ethics of decision support as a specific topic has received very little attention in comparison to the issues of privacy and other general IT ethics issues.

It is possible, however, to identify the two approaches to ethics in decision support.

4.2.1.1. *Ethics centered on the decisions made*

The first approach considers the quality of the decisions made using a DSS and their consequences, and suggests that decision makers should be alerted about the latter by the DSS itself. Mathieson [MAT 07a] proposes designing ethical decision support systems (EDSS) and describes the characteristics that these systems should possess. An EDSS should not, therefore, guide the decision maker, but rather offer a set of tools enabling them to get closer to their own ethical requirements (which they are given the credit of having).

In the same way, and making the statement that decisions made using DSS can affect a large number of stakeholders, in particular in the case of public decision-making, Chae *et al.* [CHA 05] support the idea that DSS designers must not only consider technical factors, but also consider ethical and moral factors. This is the point of view we defend in this book.

4.2.1.2. *Ethics centered on the decision-making process*

The second approach focuses on the impact the DSS can have on the *way* in which the decision is made (the decision-making process), on cognitive strategies and the structures of decision makers. Meredith and Arnott [MER 03] insist on this influence:

> [...] decision support systems [...] to a greater or lesser extent, usurp or impose structures upon the autonomy of a human decision maker. The ethical issues faced by decision support systems, therefore, are a super-set of the issues for non-autonomous information technology.

In a similar way, Chapter 3 described the risks of limiting decision-making by DSS. The objective of the methodological tool presented later in section (4.3) is to provide methodological elements to tackle this question.

4.2.1.3. *Computer ethics in the context of Big Data*

Big Data – whose characteristics were described in Chapter 2 and specific risks related were presented in Chapter 3 – generates specific ethical problems.

4.2.1.3.1. The dimensions of the ethics of Big Data

Davis and Patterson [DAV 12] identify four dimensions in Big Data ethics: identity, private life, reputation and property:

– *Identity*

Identity and the relationship that we have with this concept are called into question by Big Data. Identity can be multifaceted (professional life, association activities, musical tastes, political position, religion, friendships, etc.), but we may not necessarily want these different facets to be connected in public. As shown by Davis and Patterson, the capacity of Big Data providers to "aggregate these different facets, to correlate these different aspects of our identity – without our participation nor our consent", poses an ethical problem.

– *Privacy*

The ethical problem of respecting the private life of individuals emerges as soon as people can be identified by putting together data that are not identifier data. Indeed, 70% of US citizens can be identified when their date of birth, sex and post code are known. The near impossibility of guaranteeing anonymity quite clearly poses an ethical problem, which European countries are trying to regulate by law[5]. Davis and Patterson entertainingly illustrate this problem:

> In 1993, the New Yorker famously published a cartoon with canines at the keyboard whose caption read: "On the Internet, nobody knows you're a dog" [...]. At the time, this was funny because it was true. Today, however, in the age of prevalent Big Data, it is not only possible for people to know that you're a dog, but also what breed you are, your favorite snacks, your lineage, and whether you've ever won any awards at a dog show.

– *Reputation*

The notion of reputation has drastically changed with the Internet and the number of people who can, via the information they find, create an opinion about an individual. This effect is increased by Big Data, which can attach a set of data to one person and accumulate the data it stores over time (although these data could have disappeared from the web).

– *Ownership*

Big Data raises new types of problems of who information belongs to. Authors' rights guarantee the property of intellectual works. But can information describing a person such as their date of birth, weight, eating habits and blood pressure be assimilated to a work? On another level, does a private company have the right to *own* information about a person when this person has not given or sold it to the company?

---

5 The question, however, remains the control capacities available to public powers.

4.2.1.3.2. Ethical values

Abrams [ABR 14] proposes five ethical values that Big Data should respect:

– *Beneficial*

The value of benefit enables, on the one hand, the expected benefits and who (individuals, groups or society as a whole) benefits from this Big Data to be defined and, on the other hand, what the predictable risks are and who will bears them.

– *Progressive*

The value of progress seeks to check that the use of Big Data has a real advantage over the benefits of technologies carrying fewer risks.

– *Sustainable*

The value of sustainability is concerned with the effects of feedback mentioned in Chapter 3 and the risks they involve. A sustainable system must, therefore, be capable of managing modifications to behavior generated by its use (which was not the case during the so-called subprime mortgage crisis in 2008).

– *Respectful*

The value of respect regards the context in which data are collected and the restrictions that must be applied to its use.

– *Fair*

The final value, the value of fairness is close to the value globally used in computer ethics and mostly relates here to non-discrimination and the respect of laws.

4.2.1.3.3. Big Data and communities

Crawford *et al.* [CRA 13b] list seven points that support ethical concerns in the constitution of Big Data concerning a community of people. The first two points concern technical aspects (such as the use of Open Source tools). Two points concern the *local* level (within or close to the community): skills for Big Data must be developed locally and the property of data must remain at the local level (the community must have property of the data it generates). The final three points concern, respectively, data sharing (who will have access to the data, which must be explicitly discussed throughout the project), the right not to be sensed and the need to regularly learn from mistakes.

4.2.1.4. *Importing the principles of medical ethics*

Meredith and Arnott [MER 03] consider that the impact a DSS developer has "into the life of a decision-maker" is comparable, *mutatis mutandis*, to the impact a doctor has on their patient. They, therefore, propose drawing inspiration from the principles governing medical ethics, taking into account that, with regard to ethical questions, the domain of DSS is, in their words, "in its infancy":

– beneficence and non-maleficence;

– autonomy;

– justice.

4.2.1.4.1. The principle of beneficence and non-maleficence

Meredith and Arnott [MER 03] note that the first (double) principle of beneficence and non-maleficence can be satisfied by "removing complexity, or minimizing the effects of cognitive biases or other negative influences", though it may be accompanied by a limitation of the autonomy of the user in a "paternalistic" technical approach.

4.2.1.4.2. The principle of autonomy

Autonomy is determined by three criteria qualifying the decision, which must be:

1) intentional, the result of exercising willpower, involving the skills of the decision maker;

2) based on informed understanding;

3) free from influences that can exercise too much control over it.

DSS must be able to help when the first criterion is not (or not sufficiently) met, by improving the decision maker's ability to process the information. The second criterion, informed understanding, must be supported by the DSS by managing the evolution of the latter.

The third criterion is consistent with the Chapter 3, that presented the risk DSS carry of excessively influencing the decision-making. Meredith and Arnott [MER 03] comment that the principle of autonomy is far from being of primary importance for researchers in the domain and cite the following extract, which speaks for itself:

> Standard reports can be an asset to an organization because they limit the choice for users when it comes to researching decisions. By telling the users what they should be looking at, the designer of the standard reports *removes the burden of deciding what is important and what is not*[6] [italics for emphasis].

4.2.1.4.3. The principle of justice

This final principle can be compared with certain values (mentioned above) supported by computer ethics: equality, non-discrimination, social justice, etc. Respecting the principle of justice can result in the list and the role of the other stakeholders being modified.

4.2.2. *A reminder of the issues*

As discussed in Chapter 3, a major risk linked to the use of DSS, which is once again aggravated by Big data, is limiting the decision maker's and the organization's ability to innovate by inscribing in systems unique (and implicit) worldviews, which are reinforced by the effects of feedback and distancing from the real.

The main danger is, therefore, confusing the real with its coding, and only looking under the streetlight of the aforementioned joke (see

---

6 [CRA 99] cited by [MER 03].

Chapter 3) in the circle of digital light. Weizenbaum [WEI 76] warns us:

> Two things matter: the size of the circle of light that is the universe of one's inquiry, and the spirit of one's inquiry. The latter must include an acute awareness that there is an outer darkness, and that there are sources of illumination of which one as yet knows very little.

4.2.2.1. The position of research with regard to the issues

According to Neuman's [NEU 00] classification, there are three approaches to research. *Positivist* research is:

> an organized method for combining deductive logic with precise empirical observations of individual behavior in order to discover probabilistic causal laws that can be used to predict general patterns of human behavior.

Interpretivism (which can be compared here with constructivism) is presented as follows:

> the systematic analysis of socially meaningful interaction through the direct detailed observation of people in natural settings in order to arrive at understandings and interpretations of how people create and maintain their social worlds.

Finally, the *critical* approach:

> goes beyond surface illusions to reveal underlying structures and conflicts of social relations as a way to empower people to improve the social world.

Our approach involves critical research. This orientation remains relatively uncommon in research into IT systems, as noted by Rowe [ROW 09]. Stahl [STA 08a] comments "there is an intrinsic link between ethics and critical research" and continues by stressing the need for critical researchers to specify on which ethical premises they are based.

To present these premises, we will use Ricœur [RIC 98] who establishes a distinction between *ethics* and *morals*. He reserves the term *ethics* for "any questioning that predates the introduction of the idea of moral law" and calls moral "anything concerning good and bad relating to laws, rules and imperatives". We will retain the idea of a chain which spans from the most generic ethical principles to the most applicable moral imperatives, or, according to Ricœur [RIC 98], which reconstructs "all the intermediaries between freedom, which is the point of departure, and law, which is the point of arrival".

Therefore, at the highest level is the freedom to act, the "ability to call oneself the author of one's own actions" [RIC 00]. Researchers have this freedom, as do IT system designers, who we consider *responsible* (or co-responsible) for respecting ethical principles and moral rules in the operation of the IT system. It is to be stressed that all the other stakeholders in the organization also have this freedom.

Geoff Walsham entitled one of his recent articles "Are We Making a Better World with ICTs?". Our research has the modest yet deliberate aim of improving the world in which we live. We believe *democracy* is the best value to achieve this ambition.

4.2.2.2. *The value of democracy*

The main ethical value we seek to support is democracy. For us, this value assumes a paradigmatic status. We place it at the top of the hierarchy of ethical values; respecting democracy results in a series of other values being respected.

Our aim is, therefore, to help the production of IT systems, and in particular DSS, which respects the requirements of democracy. Democracy is considered above all else to *guarantee access to a plurality of worldviews*. Unlike most computer ethics approaches on the topic, democracy, for us, does not therefore focus on giving a voice to groups or individuals, although we do include the principle of respecting the interests of each stakeholder.

Supporting greater democracy in organizations can, in our opinion, support the long-term development of the organization and, more generally, sustainable development for the society. It involves fighting against what, in organizations' IS, can hinder innovation, particularly in decision-making. Supporting democracy requires, in particular, discovering in the IS what makes it possible to impose a *unique* view of objects, players, categories and so on.

For public institutions, the promotion of democracy strives to identify, within public action tools, the political choices hidden within the IT tools. These choices are not debated by local representatives, rather they are imposed on them [LAS 05]. This case, therefore, concerns supporting a reinvestment in politics by local representatives.

4.2.2.3. *The need to assist the responsibility of designers*

As said previously, the designer of IT systems and DSS must be "the author of [their] own actions", and therefore responsible. Our position is that this ability to act, this (moral as well as economic and social) responsibility must be *assisted*.

4.2.3. *Design phases to be favored*

Mathieson [MAT 07a] stresses the difficulty of designing ethical DSS:

> We cannot define ethical decision methods precisely. The process should change with task difficulty, decision maker personality and mindfulness, group norms, cultural differences, and so on.

In our opinion, ethical values must be included within the DSS engineering process and must not be the object of a specific method. At what point should we start to be concerned about ethical values? Detweiler and Harbers [DET 14] believe that it should be considered in the early phases:

> A system's impact on human values often is not considered until the system has been put to use and its desirable and/or undesirable consequences have come to

light. [...] A system's impact on human values need not be an afterthought; rather, relevant values should be considered early during design, when a system is still malleable.

Moreover, it is considered that supporting the value of democracy implies that the methodological tools proposed to include this ethical value support *dialog* between the designers and the other stakeholders (who, remember, are equally responsible for the values included in IT systems and DSS). In the process of designing an IT system or a DSS, certain phases require, more than others, cooperation between all stakeholders and are, therefore, more suited to such a dialogue, in particular in the requirements definition, testing and implementation phases.

Our research focuses on the first of these phases – requirements engineering – and thereby coincides with Detweiler and Harbers' concern.

The objective of requirements engineering is to determine the features of the future system and the constraints it must respect, as well as to reposition the global objective of the system in relation to the general end purposes of the organization. Studying the system's global objective and the organization's end purposes is the object of *early requirements*, which unfortunately remains a poorly equipped phase at the conceptual and methodological levels [REG 03]. This phase is, however, essential with regard to the economic and social responsibility of the designer, as it will *set* the aforementioned macro level (paradigms, the organization's view of its world, players, objects, etc.) which will constitute the framework in which the features and then the technical characteristics of the DSS will be inscribed.

From the perspective of respecting the value of democracy, our contribution aims to facilitate the co-construction of early requirements between the different stakeholders or, at least, to enable the choices made at this level and their consequences on the system to be made *explicit*. We have chosen to enrich the conceptual interfaces used by the designers and the other stakeholders to limit the number of implicit choices as far as possible. Indeed, implicit choices, which can concern all levels (from the macro to micro via all intermediaries), are one of the sources of the "automatic" integration of ethical or "unethical" values in IT systems and DSS without being the object of debate.

4.2.4. *Conclusion*

To conclude this section, it could be said that our objective is to equip the "ability to act" (the responsibility) of IT system and DSS designers (in collaboration with the other stakeholders) while the IT system and DSS are being developed, such that these systems support, in turn, stakeholders' "ability to act" in their activities within the organization. Our research is, therefore, an *engineering of responsibility*.

4.3. Our contribution to an engineering of responsibility

This section presents a model used to assist the definition of early requirements from the perspective of democracy, which is, in our opinion, a generic value. This model reveals the chain spanning from the representations (paradigm, ontological level and macro level) to the norms (micro level) via an intermediary level (principles).

It can be used in two configurations: to analyze an existing situation and/or to build an alternative. It can, therefore, help understand how some values are integrated in IT systems and DSS and it can also help promote other values by ensuring they are expressed at each of the three levels.

This methodological tool is one component of a complete requirements engineering method for DSS design, which considers the economic and social responsibility of the designer. For details of this method, refer to [SAL 13a].

The content of the model will first be presented and then an application of the model will be proposed for illustration purposes.

4.3.1. *The doxai, principles and norms (DPN) model*

This model identifies and makes explicit three levels to express the values of the organization: the level of doxai, the level of principles and the level of norms (see Figure 4.1).

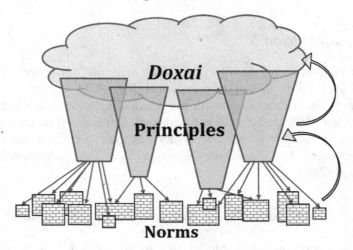

Figure 4.1. *Global diagram of the DPN model*

4.3.1.1. *Doxai*

The first level, the *doxai* level, relates to the worldviews existing in the organization (macro level): the ontological status of the large objects involved in the organization, paradigmatic choices, broad strategic options or policies. The options taken at this level (most often in an implicit and even tacit manner) prescribe the *sense* that will be embodied in the IS and, particularly, the broad ethical values that will or will not be respected.

The second part of this section will present an example of the application of the DPN model including the description of two doxai. We will thus limit ourselves here to three examples.

The first example is the overall doxai on economy and social issues. One doxa separates the economy from social issues, whereas another doxa considers them to be absolutely inseparable. It should be noted that our work subscribes entirely to this second doxa, and treats economic and social responsibility as an entity that cannot be dissociated.

A second example is the enterprise. The enterprise can be considered, as shareholder theory (described above) holds, a system whose *raison d'être* is to produce share value (we could nowadays add: as quickly as possible). It is, therefore, seen as a liquid asset whose longevity is not particularly sought. Another representation of the enterprise can perceive it to be a system whose mission is to produce goods and services.

The third example concerns representations of the territory (for example, for a territorial authority), which were mentioned in Chapter 3. A first doxa considers the territory as *given* (postulated), and it is, therefore, seen as a finite space demarcated by borders. A second doxa considers the territory as having to be created during a project coordinating players that are spatially close. The project and the territory, therefore, cannot be separated (a territory can only exist through a series of projects).

4.3.1.2. Principles

Doxai are general views that cannot be used to organize and check the organization's activities; more structured devices are required.

Principles specify with which concepts, which objects and which methods the orientations of the previous level will be made more operational. Principles structure organizations (of all sizes) and their actions. As will be seen, principles produce norms. We will call principles *machines for producing norms* [SAL 13a].

At this level, we find:

– methods for defining the mission and the perimeter of the organization in question;

– the global objectives (unquantified) assigned to the organization;

– methods for treating the stakeholders in a project (methods for determining the list of stakeholders, their hierarchy, their attributions, etc.);

– management methods: decision-making methods, global organization methods, methods for organizing processes, types of relationships with players external to the organization, principles determining the internal rules, etc.;

– the logic of analytical accounting;

– the logic of criteria for investment selection;

– methods for defining evaluation indicators, etc.

These principles are embodied in IT systems and DSS and their governance:

– definition of the IT system's missions, of its perimeter (including or not including players external to the organization);

– methods for designing and governing IT systems and DSS;

– the structures of IT systems and DSS: conceptual models for data, processing and interfaces, and dimensions retained in data warehouses;

– principles of dividing decisions and actions between the user (or the decision maker user) and the application;

– methods for calculating indicators (including quantification conventions), their interpretation, defining the thresholds of automatic action implementation;

– the principle of checking employee's activities in real time, etc.

It is noted that in the literature, the level of principles is rarely mentioned as it is confused with the next level (norms). However, for us, it represents the main space for expressing democracy or the prevention of democracy. More generally, the majority of ethical (or "unethical") values are integrated in IT systems at this level.

The aforementioned representations for the enterprise and the territory bring about different principles depending on the doxa adopted, resulting in the value of democracy being considered differently.

In the first representation of the enterprise, the structure of the IS reflects the splitting of the organization into centers of profit. Analytical accounting is organized according to the logic of the result (costs and margin). The focus is globally on financial information, financial ratios and the evolution of share value. The design and the governance of IT systems involve a very limited number of stakeholders whose roles are very restricted.

In the second representation, the IT system is a space for consolidating/memorizing knowledge. It must help identify the evolution of fundamental needs. Analytical accounting is organized around the production of added value [BRO 13]. In the design of IT systems and their governance, the rights of different stakeholders are comparable.

At the level of economic development policies, the two views of the territory produce totally different and even opposing action logics [SAL 10]. For the first doxa (which considers the territory as given, equipped with finite resources), actions are centered on the enterprise. Whereas for the second doxa (for which the territory is created as a result of projects and for which these relationships should therefore be reinforced), they are centered on the inter-relationships between players. The IT system expresses one or the other of these logics via the entities considered in the conceptual models. In the case of the first representation of the territory, the IT system may not include in its conceptual models any information about the relationships between players, making any policy change difficult if not impossible.

4.3.1.3. Norms

For us, a *norm* is anything that concretely organizes the way people act within organizations. It is the level of the tangible expression of ethical values (or lack thereof). It is produced by the application of the principles, models and methods of the previous level:

– management methods will, for instance, result in the organization of specific working hours (flexi time, annualization of working time, work in multi-shift operations, etc.), management procedures, concrete decision processes (list of the types of participants in the decision-making, information to be collected, deadline, evaluation, etc.), the accounts for analytical accounting, etc.;

– these norms will be coded in IT systems and DSS: software including the organization of work and procedures, software monitoring activity in real time, predesigned cubes in data warehouses, dashboards with quantified indicators, list of criteria (classification and selection), etc.

This third level (micro level) is the most visible, and consequently it is often the only level that is considered in approaches to computer ethics.

At the level of norms, the DSS of the enterprise considered according to the first doxa will present financial ratios and indicators measuring costs, and the IT system will produce software monitoring employees by the means of restrictive procedures (all destined to reduce costs), etc. In the second representation, the IT system will calculate the added value available, will measure the positive externalities (innovation, etc.) and negative externalities (pollution, etc.) and so on.

IT systems serving a territory's economic development policy will include, for example, different selection criteria for application documents depending on the two views of the territory. For the first view, the perimeter of these criteria is the enterprise, and for the second view, the perimeter will be expanded to include enterprise clusters and other players.

4.3.2. Applying the DPN model for evaluation

The model, which was succinctly presented above, can be applied to a number of types of objects and concepts that are involved in the life of organizations. To support the implementation of the aforementioned method, a number of entities have been subject to double DPN modeling. The dominant representation of the object was modeled, and then an alternative representation was built. The *enterprise* [SAL 13b], the *labor*, the *territory*, the *resources of a territory*, etc., were then modeled to the three levels of DPN according to the dominant doxa and then according to an alternative view.

We will now briefly illustrate the use of the DPN model for the evaluation of the employees within organizations (public or private), by presenting two competing representations of this concept.

4.3.2.1. *Two doxai about evaluation*

For a first doxa, the intention of evaluation is to check the conformity of a target or a predefined model. This doxa considers differences to be frictions, to be eliminated. It aims for homogeneity. It holds that everything can be quantified and compared and that as the real exists in an immanent way, quantifications quantify what exists (the real) in an objective, neutral and technical manner. As such, quantification cannot be debated (thus, standing against the value of democracy). The activity of manager will consist mostly of comparing, categorizing, selecting, rewarding/punishing (and watching). This doxa, based on control (and not trust), relates to the figure of *homo economicus* (calculating and egotistical) and promotes competition as the only way for people as well as organizations, territories, states, etc., to have relationships [MET 10].

It should be noted that this doxa, which emerged from private enterprises, has expanded today to the voluntary sector, institutions (including universities), public services and States. Le Galès [LEG 05], talking about evaluation, by the State, of the policies of territorial authorities in the United Kingdom, notes that: "in terms of relationship with society, this implicit theorization is not built upon the dynamics of mobilization or cooperation, but of the constraints of an optimum management model whose aims are never laid out nor discussed".

In a second representation of evaluation, the intention is to identify skills (or lack thereof) and knowledge, so that they can be developed and promoted. This doxa considers that not everything can be reduced to digital values (likewise not every value can be compared to a monetary value), and that not everything is comparable (thus, promoting the notion of incomparability). Reality is seen as a construction, and its quantification presupposes prior equivalence conventions [DES 03]. Evaluation can involve activities other than quantification. Managing will, therefore, be identifying differences, looking for complementarities, latencies, emergences and looking toward the future. This representation of evaluation recognizes diversity as the only source of evolution. It is based on trust (in the capacities of each individual or group of individuals), and trust is seen as an essential element for the development of any type of organization. This second doxa is better suited to respecting the value of democracy.

4.3.2.2. *A number of principles that embody the two doxai*

As a large number of principles exist, we will only provide a few examples.

At the level of management principles, the first doxa organizes a fragmented (rather than systemic) evaluation of employees (individual evaluation) and costs (the elements of costs are seen to be independent from each other). The types of indicators are decided by management alone (and sometimes only by senior management). The same is true for the definition of limit values, standard interpretations, etc. IT systems and DSS include these principles by defining the structure of data, programs enabling the automatic collection of data, the automatic calculation of indicators and standard interpretations and the automatic implementation of actions from certain values.

Implementing these principles may stand against respecting ethical values. Studying UK public institutions, Le Galès [LEG 05] observes that "every expense, every program must be committed to the cost/effectiveness ratio and no other criterion, which requires the production of indicators, performance, evaluation and competition measures" and comments that these principles contradict the previously existing principles which, for public markets, selected enterprises according to criteria including social, moral or political aspects (enterprises working with South Africa at the time of apartheid were thus divided from the markets of certain authorities). This tendency of drastically limiting the number of selection criteria or evaluation indicators, thus resulting in a unique criterion or indicator, also exists in enterprises.

In the second representation of evaluation, the organization is considered to be a *system* (rather than a sum of parts). Evaluation is applied to groups and is conducted dynamically (and therefore systematically measures the evolutions). Evaluation methods, either quantitative or qualitative, are debated by the stakeholders in question. The IT system provides a skills map and its evolution over time. The engineering of software collecting data, calculating indicators and constituting dashboards, more generally DSS, includes the stakeholders.

4.3.2.3. *Some examples of norms operationalizing these principles*

Norms will make evaluation principles operational. As there is a lot of norms, we will provide only a few examples here.

From the first representation, norms will, for example, result in DSS presenting the scores of employees (or enterprises, or even States), as well as assisting the selection of a particular investment, a particular employee or even the decision of whether to launch a particular project. Lorrain [LOR 05] notes that "the discount rate and its duration chosen for a large equipment project will make it realizable or not" or that "redemption periods result at the end of the chain in tariffs paid by users".

Remember that indicators, which are the norm *par excellence*, bring about considerable effects of feedback, particularly in the case where the evaluation method is exclusively quantitative and decided by management alone without a real debate with the employees being evaluated.

Norms of the second representation produce dashboards showing evaluation results which are not exclusively quantitative, proposing selection criteria with multiple aims. In this representation, DSS are not the only decision support tools and consultation and discussion can also be used to make a final choice.

Conclusion: key points for DSS design

Ethics: an approach neglected by IT system and DSS specialists

In the domains of both IT systems and DSS, there are very few publications about ethics in the major journals of the discipline. Training for future IT system or DSS designers very rarely includes ethics. Yet the generalization of IT systems to all organizations and all activities (especially decision-making), which comes alongside a financialized orientation of the economy, raises a growing number of increasingly severe ethical problems.

A concern dating from the dawn of cybernetics

This lack of interest corresponds to a strong tendency in research into IT systems and DSS (which is often borne testament in the history of the discipline), which tends to neglect organizational and, more generally, human aspects to focus on purely technical questions. The first 30 years of computing did, however, see the development, within the domain itself, of a critical point of view and a reflection on the need to discuss and decide the domains where computing could (or could not) be applied. Many papers from this period remain relevant today.

The need to assist ethical requirement with methodological tools

Work into computer ethics is mostly conducted by philosophers and is not, in the majority of cases, easy for IT system or DSS designers to use. However, for a number of years, a real effort has been made to propose methodological tools adapted to the design of IT systems and DSS. A typical example of this is the *value sensitive design* (VSD) method.

The work of the operationalization of computer ethics must, however, be continued and particularly focus on the specificities of DSS design.

The analysis of early requirements, key phase in the consideration of alternative worldviews

The first stage of requirements engineering, early requirements analysis, will set the general worldviews that will structure the entire DSS. Generally, not very well equipped in IT system and DSS engineering methods, this phase is not specifically dealt with by computer ethics. It is, however, the output of this phase, the general representations chosen, that will provide the ethical values that will or will not be included in the system.

A central ethical value for DSS: democracy

The values supported by computer ethics are of very varied levels; it is difficult to recognize a general organization, if it were a simple hierarchy, among these values. In our opinion, *democracy* is a generic value from which other values ensue. We understand democracy as being the preservation of a diversity of worldviews within the organization, thereby guaranteeing the ability of the latter to innovate.

A methodological tool to deal with the worldviews integrated into DSS

The DPN model is a methodological tool aimed at supporting the work of making explicit the ethical values incorporated into a system, as well as organizing the integration of a given value at different levels (D, P and N), finally enabling its operationalization. This initial tool must, of course, be refined and completed so as to move toward the development of a real engineering of responsibility.

General Conclusion

DSS, one of the components of the global decision-making system

Decision support system (DSS) can sometimes greatly help improve the decisions that are made. However, it should not be forgotten that DSS only have a sense within the global decision-making system, which also comprises of the decision maker who uses the DSS to make a decision in an organizational environment [SPR 82]. At the center of the system are the decision maker and the knowledge enabling them to understand the decision situation, and the organization, which constitutes the end purpose of the system. The DSS is a tool to serve them.

However, there is a risk that has on occasion been recognized, of the hierarchy of these components being reversed. Frequently put at the center of the system, the DSS therefore produces its own end purposes (through the world views it includes) and frames the ways of defining, qualifying and structuring the problems requiring decision-making.

Yet, the definition of the end purposes of a system (the decision-making system, or more globally, the complex system formed by an organization), is an activity of *producing sense*, which requires the ability to judge rather than to simply calculate.

Judgment or calculation?

Weizenbaum entitled his major work "Computer Power and Human Reason. From judgment to calculation" [WEI 76], thus putting in opposition reason and the power of computers, judgment and calculation. This distinction relates to that drawn by Stiegler [STI 14], who, using Kant, separated understanding, which is analytical and can be transformed into calculation, from reason, which collects its data from experience or intuition such as to make decisions.

This opposition can also be found between the two decision theories. Normative theory, which sees decision-making as the optimum calculation of a utility function, stands in opposition to engineering theory, which considers decision-making to be a complete process including the definition of the problem, and assumes that no optimum exists, but only a *satisficing* decision.

This distinction, which draws a border between what can and cannot be automated, should be compared to the categories of decisions depending on their degree of structure. Well-structured decisions, which correspond to well-known problems, only require understanding and can be the object of a calculation. Besides, their status as decisions should itself be questioned, as a decision involves a choice between a number of options. Weakly or unstructured decisions, particularly those needing to tackle undefined problems, require, conversely, the engagement of the reason, of the judgment of decision makers. The use of one calculation to deal with this type of decision incurs the significant risk of "type III" errors [MIT 93], which result in solving the wrong problem precisely.

Preserving the diversity of knowledge

The evolution of our societies, and particularly the impact of our activities on a space covering the planet, in a temporal horizon going well beyond that of our lifetimes, multiplies unknown problems involving a very large number of dimensions. These problems require complex decision-making.

It is therefore central to preserve, as far as possible, the option for decision makers to call upon knowledge being varied in its content, form or vehicle. It is also essential not to create a confusion between the different levels formed by data (without sense), information (contextualized, carrying sense) and knowledge (inscribed in an intention, creating sense and enabling action). Knowledge, a complex result of experience, values and intuition, requires a human subject who is in essence endowed with intention. All these requirements fix an impassable border between knowledge, the prerogative of humans (or living beings) and what digital processing can produce, however sophisticated it is.

What digitization can't code[1]

Though a digital system cannot create sense, it can help the decision maker to interpret a situation through a set of data (by presenting it in different axes, comparing it to other data, aggregating it, sometimes realizing advanced calculations). But it can also restrict this interpretation (through the representations inscribed in the IT system or the DSS, which code some objects and some of their characteristics and leave others uncoded, use some types of processing and not others, etc.). This is particularly true in cases, which are increasing in organizations, where the IT system constitutes an almost unique source of information for decision makers.

However, digitization, though it can code everything, does so at the sometimes exorbitant price of drastically reducing the real. Decision-making based exclusively on digital data, in the illusion that it provides an exhaustive or sufficient representation of the real, runs the risk of defining problems in a truncated and biased way. Though it is essential that, faced with unknown situations that can be extremely complex in the case of public decision making, decision makers use a variety of sources of information, the question of digitizing the real goes beyond this one, important issue.

---

1 Paraphrasing the title of M. Sandel's [SAN 12] work: "What money can't buy".

In our opinion, it is imperative that the question be asked, in organizations and probably beyond, of what can be the object of digital coding and processing and what should not. This concern obviously contradicts the current dynamic of digital technology development, which is leading to the unrestricted production of digital equivalents of all elements of human life across all domains. We think it a good idea to return to simple questioning in the same vein of Weizenbaum [WEI 76] who commented: "we can count, but we are rapidly forgetting how to say what is worth counting and why."

Though everything has the potential to be digitally coded, just like money has the potential to buy everything, it is worth questioning: to what end should coding be operated, to obtain what result with the data produced, what part of the real is lost in coding (and how can we preserve access to this uncoded part), what are the effects of feedback that coding could have on the real and, beyond that, can coding itself destroy what is coded? Similarly, the image of an imperfect human (irrational, dominated by their emotions, limited by their memory and ability to calculate, etc.) that digital technology (perfect and neutral) would "augment" without loss nor risk should, in our opinion, be debated.

If we apply to digitization what Michael Sandel [SAN 12] proposes for the market, we ought to "rethink the role and reach" of digitization "in our social practices, human relationships, and everyday lives". Due to the sometimes considerable consequences of certain decisions, this suggestion is particularly vital for decision-making and systems built to support it.

What can we do?

Throughout this book, we have insisted on the need to guarantee DSS are inscribed with diverse world views, points of view and ways of reasoning, to preserve as far as is possible organizations' ability to innovate. The moral as well as economic and social responsibility of DSS designers has been stressed. We have also emphasized that designers share this responsibility with all the stakeholders in a DSS project. Finally, we have confessed that calling on this responsibility can only be legitimate if it is assisted and equipped by means of a real *engineering of responsibility.*

Approaches have been proposed and a methodological tool has been presented and illustrated. This initial work must be continued in a pluridisciplinary approach with the aim of producing operational results which can be used by designers and other stakeholders in their interactions.

In the same vein, training for decision system should, in our opinion, include teaching about computer ethics for DSS and a reflection on the influences these systems can have on the decision process and its results.

Finally, and more generally, it is important (and relatively urgent) that an epistemological reflection be conducted within the domain of DSS. In our opinion, the fact that a new field, which combines mathematics, statistics and computing, is called "data science" reveals that there has been no real reflection about the aforementioned questions concerning the relationship between the data and what it codes. It therefore also seems appropriate that computer science training (including that for "data scientists") should include teaching from domains where there has been a reflection on these topics (for instance sociology for survey methods) as well as teaching about epistemology.

Bibliography

[ABR 14] ABRAMS M., *A Unified Ethical Frame for Big Data Analysis*, The Information Accountability Foundation, 2014.

[ADI 03] ADIT (Agence pour la Diffusion de l'Information Technologique), *Synthèse des 1ères Assises de l'intelligence territoriale*, Deauville, November 24, 2003.

[ALC 04] ALCARAS J.-R., "Les conceptions de la décision en sciences économiques: vers une approche ingénieriale?", in ALCARAS J.-R., GIANFALDONI P., PACHÉ G. (eds), *Décider dans les organisations – Dialogues critiques entre économie et gestion*, L'Harmattan, Paris, pp. 57–78, 2004.

[ALC 11] ALCARAS J.-R., "Les théories économiques de la décision à l'épreuve de la quantification – Quand symboliser n'est pas forcément quantifier!", *Nouvelles Perspectives en Sciences Sociales* (NPSS), vol. 6, no. 2, pp. 161–194, 2011.

[ALT 80] ALTER S.L., *Decision Support Systems: Current Practice and Continuing Challenge*, Addison-Wesley, Reading, MA, 1980.

[AND 08] ANDERSON C.H., "The end of theory: the data deluge makes the scientific method obsolete", *Wired Magazine*, 16 July 2008.

[ANS 88] ANSOFF H.I., *The New Corporate Strategy*, Wiley, New York, 1988.

[ANT 65] ANTHONY R.N., *Planning and Control Systems: a Framework for Analysis*, Harvard University Graduate School of Business Administration, Cambridge, MA, 1965.

[ANT 96] ANTÓN A.I., "Goal-based requirements analysis", *Proceedings of the 2nd International Conference of Requirement Engineering* (ICRE'96), pp. 136–144, 1996.

[ANZ 86] ANZIEU D., MARTIN J.-Y., *La dynamique des groupes restreint*, 8th ed., Presses Universitaires de France, Paris, 1986.

[ARD 13] ARDUIN P.-E., GRUNDSTEIN M., ROSENTHAL-SABROUX C., "From knowledge sharing to collaborative decision making", *International Journal of Information and Decision Sciences*, vol. 5, no. 3, pp. 295–311, 2013.

[ARI 14] ARISTOTLE, *Nicomachean Ethics*, Written 350 B.C.E, Translated by W. D. Ross, The University of Adelaide Library, Adelaide, Australia, 2014.

[ARN 08a] ARNOTT D., DODSON G., "Decision support systems failure", in BURSTEIN F., HOLSAPPLE C.W. (eds), *Handbook on Decision Support Systems 1*, Springer Verlag, Berlin, Heidelberg, pp. 763–790, 2008.

[ARN 08b] ARNOTT D., PERVAN G., "Eight key issues for the decision support systems discipline", *Decision Support Systems*, vol. 44, pp. 657–672, 2008.

[ATL 14] ATLAN H., *Croyances. Comment expliquer le monde?*, Éditions Autrement, 2014.

[AZA 12] AZADEH A., SABERI M., JIRYAEI Z., "An intelligent decision support system for forecasting and optimization of complex personnel attributes in a large bank", *Expert Systems with Applications*, vol. 39, no. 16, pp. 12358–12370, 15 November 2012.

[BAR 10] BARONE D., YU E., WON J. *et al.*, "Enterprise modeling for business intelligence", in VAN BOMMEL P. (ed.), *The Practice of Enterprise Modeling*, PoEM 2010, LNBIP 68, pp. 31–45, 2010.

[BAR 14] BARONE D., PEYTON L., RIZZOLO F. *et al.*, "Model-based management of strategic initiatives", *Journal on Data Semantics*, pp. 1–17, July 2014.

[BAT 72] BATESON G., *Steps to an Ecology of Mind*, Chandler Pub. Co., San Francisco, 1972.

[BAU 82] BAUMOL W.J., "Contestable markets: an uprising in the theory of industry structure", *American Economic Review*, vol. 72, no. 1, pp. 1–15, March 1982.

[BEL 04] BELL F., ADAM A., "The problem of integrating ethics into IS practice", *Proceedings of the 13th European Conference on Information Systems (ECIS)*, Finland, pp. 189–199, 2004.

[BEL 13] BELLATRECHE L., KHOURI S., BERKANI N., "Semantic data warehouse design: from ETL to deployment à la Carte", in MENG W., FENG L., BRESSAN S. *et al.* (eds), *Database Systems for Advanced Applications*, Lecture Notes in Computer Science, vol. 7826, pp. 64–83, 2013.

[BÉN 08] BÉNABEN F., HANACHI C., LAURAS M. *et al.*, "A metamodel and its ontology to guide crisis characterization and its collaborative management", in FIEDRICH F., VAN DE WALLE B. (eds), *Proceedings of the 5th International ISCRAM Conference*, Washington, DC, pp. 189–196, 2008.

[BER 83] BERRY M., Une Technologie invisible? L'impact des instruments de gestion sur l'évolution des systèmes humains, Centre de recherche en gestion (CRG) de l'École Polytechnique, Paris, 1983.

[BHA 07] BHARGAVA H.K., POWER D.J., SUN D., "Progress in web-based decision support technologies", *Decision Support Systems*, vol. 43, no. 4, pp. 1083–1095, August 2007.

[BIT 11] BITTERER A., SCHLEGEL K., LANEY D., "Predicts 2012: business intelligence still subject to nontechnical challenges", *Gartner*, ID: G00227192, 13 December 2011.

[BOE 88] BOEHM B.W., "A spiral model of software development and enhancement", *IEEE Computer*, vol. 21, no. 5, pp. 61–72, 1988.

[BOE 10] BOERBOOM L.G.L., "Integrating spatial planning and decision support system infrastructure and spatial data infrastructure", *Proceedings of the GSDI 12 World Conference*, Singapore, 19–22 October 2010.

[BÖH 00] BÖHNLEIN M., ULBRICH VOM ENDE A., "Business process oriented development of data warehouse structures", in *Proceedings of Data Warehousing 2000*, Heidelberg, Germany, Physica Verlag, 2000.

[BOL 87] BOLTANSKI L., *Les cadres. La formation d'un groupe social*, Minuit, Paris, 1982. *The Making of a Class. Cadres in French Society*, Cambridge University Press, Cambridge, UK, 1987.

[BOL 08] BOLLECKER M., MATHIEU P., CLEMENTZ C., "L'évolution des systèmes de gestion face aux enjeux de la responsabilité sociale: le cas de la comptabilité et du contrôle de gestion", *Gestion 2000*, vol. 4, pp. 49–65, 2008.

[BOR 08] BORNING A., WADDELL P., FORSTER R., "Urbansim: using simulation to inform public deliberation and decision-making", in CHEN H., BRANDT L., GREGG V. *et al.* (eds), *Digital Government: E-Government Research, Case Studies, and Implementation*, Springer-Verlag, pp. 439–463, 2008.

[BOR 09] BORGIDA A., MYLOPOULOS J., "A sophisticate's guide to information modeling", in JEUSFELD M.A., JARKE M., MYLOPOULOS J. (eds), *Metamodeling for Method Engineering*, MIT Press, pp. 1–41, 2009.

[BOY 99] BOYDENS I., *Informatique, normes et temps*, Bruylant, Brussels, 1999.

[BRE 10] BREY PH., "Values in technology and disclosive computer ethics", in FLORIDI L. (ed.), *The Cambridge Handbook of Information and Computer Ethics*, Cambridge University Press, pp. 41–58, 2010.

[BRO 86] BROOKS F.P., "No silver bullet – essence and accidents of software engineering", in KUGLER H.-J. (ed.), *Proceedings of the IFIP 10th World Computing Conference*, Elsevier Science B.V., Amsterdam, pp. 1069–1076, 1986.

[BRO 13] BRODIER P.-L., "La logique de la valeur ajoutée, une autre façon de compter", *L'Expansion Management Review*, no. 148, pp. 20–27, 2013.

[BUR 09] BURGEMEESTRE B., LIU J., HULSTIJN J. *et al.*, "Early requirements engineering for e-customs decision support: assessing overlap in mental models", *Proceedings of CAiSE Forum*, pp. 31–36, 2009.

[BYN 85] BYNUM T.W., "Computers and ethics", *Metaphilosophy*, vol. 16, no. 4, pp. 263–377, October 1985.

[CAH 04] CAHIER J.P., ZAHER L.H., LEBOEUF J.P. *et al.*, "Une expérience de co-construction de "carte de thèmes" dans le domaine des logiciels libres", *Colloque En route vers Lisbonne*, Luxembourg, 12–13 October 2004.

[CHA 05] CHAE B., PARADICE D., COURTNEY J.F. *et al.*, "Incorporating an ethical perspective into problem formulation: implications for decision support systems design", *Decision Support Systems*, vol. 40, pp. 197–212, 2005.

[CHE 12] CHEN H., CHIANG R.H.L., STOREY V.C., "Business intelligence and analytics: from big data to big impact", *MIS Quarterly*, vol. 36, no. 4, pp. 1165–1188, December 2012.

[CHU 99] CHUNG L., NIXON B.A., YU E. *et al.*, *Non-Functional Requirements in Software Engineering*, Kluwer Academic Publishers, 1999.

[CIG 13] CIGREF, Identification et gouvernance des enjeux éthiques émergents dans les systèmes d'information (IDEGOV), 2013.

[COL 93] COLLETIS G., PECQUEUR B., "Intégration des espaces et quasi-intégration des firmes: vers de nouvelles rencontres productives?", in BELLET M., COLLETIS G., ET LUNG Y. (eds) *Economie de proximités*, *Revue d'Économie Régionale et Urbaine*, no. 3, pp. 489–508, 1993.

[COL 08] COLLETIS G., DIEUAIDE P., "Travail, compétences et nouvelle centralité du rapport salarial", in COLLETIS G., PAULRÉ B. (eds), *Les nouveaux horizons du capitalisme. Pouvoirs, valeurs et temps*, Economica, Paris, pp. 99–124, 2008.

[COL 10] COLLETIS G., Rapport de mutation 2: Vers une stratégie régionale en faveur des activités transversales, Report, Région Midi-Pyrénées, June 2010.

[CON 01] CONKLIN J., *Wicked Problems and Social Complexity*, CogNexus Institute, 2001.

[COT 00] COTTONE R.R., CLAUS R.E., "Ethical decision-making models: a review of the literature", *Journal of Counselling & Development*, vol. 78, pp. 275–283, 2000.

[COU 01] COURTNEY J.F., "Decision making and knowledge management in inquiring organizations: toward a new decision-making paradigm for DSS", *Decision Support Systems*, vol. 31, no. 1, pp. 17–38, 2001.

[CRA 99] CRAIG R.S., VIVONA J., BERCOVICH D., *Microsoft Data Warehousing: Building Distributed Decision Support Systems*, Wiley, Toronto, Canada, 1999.

[CRA 13a] CRAWFORD K., "The hidden biases in big data", *Harvard Business Review*, available at https://hbr.org/2013/04/the-hidden-biases-in-big-data, April 2013.

[CRA 13b] CRAWFORD K., FALEIROS G., LUERS A. *et al.*, Big data, communities and ethical resilience: a framework for action, white paper, Bellagio/PopTech Fellows, 2013.

[CYE 63] CYERT R.M., MARCH J.G., *A Behavioral Theory of the Firm*, Prentice-Hall, Englewood Cliffs, N.J., 1963.

[DAN 61] DANIEL D.R., "Management information crisis", *Harvard Business Review*, vol. 35, no. 9, pp. 111–121, September–October 1961.

[DAV 98] DAVENPORT T.H., PRUSAK L., *Working Knowledge How Organizations Manage What They Know*, Harvard Business School Press, Boston, 1998.

[DAV 99] DAVENPORT T.H., "Privilégier l'information sur la technologie", *Supplément Les Échos: L'art du management de l'information*, 1st October 1999.

[DAV 12] DAVIS K., PATTERSON D., *Ethics of Big Data*, O'Reilly Media, 2012.

[DEM 13] DEMIRKAN H., DURSUN D., "Leveraging the capabilities of service-oriented decision support systems: putting analytics and big data in cloud", *Decision Support Systems*, vol. 55, no. 1, pp. 412–421, April 2013.

[DES 98] DESROSIÈRES A., *The Politics of Large Numbers: a History of Statistical Reasoning*, Harvard University Press, Cambridge, MA, 1998.

[DES 03] DESROSIÈRES A., "Du réalisme des objets de la comptabilité nationale", *Congrès de l'Association Française de Sciences Économiques*, Paris, 2003.

[DES 12] DESROSIÈRES A., "Est-il bon, est-il méchant? Le rôle du nombre dans le gouvernement de la cité néolibérale", *Nouvelles perspectives en sciences sociales* (NPSS), vol. 7, no. 2, pp. 261–295, May 2012.

[DET 14] DETWEILER C., HARBERS M., "Value stories: putting human values into requirements engineering", *Proceedings of Workshop on Creativity in Requirements Engineering (CreaRE)*, 2014.

[DEW 10] DEWEY J., *How We Think*, Health & Co, Boston, 1910.

[ELH 11] EL HADDADI A., Fouille multidimensionnelle sur les données textuelles visant à extraire les réseaux sociaux et sémantiques pour leur exploitation via la téléphonie mobile, PhD Thesis, University of Toulouse III, 2011.

[FAY 96] FAYYAD U.M., PIATESKY-SHAPIRO G., SMYTH P. *et al.*, "From data mining to knowledge discovery: an overview", in FAYYAD U.M., PIATETSKY-SHAPIRO G., SMYTH P. *et al.* (eds), *Advances in Knowledge Discovery and Data Mining*, AAAI Press/The MIT Press, Menlo Park, pp. 1–36, 1996.

[FER 05] FERNANDEZ A., *Les nouveaux tableaux de bord des managers*, Les Éditions d'Organisation, Paris, 2005.

[FIN 05] FINLAY P.N., *Introducing Decision Support Systems*, Blackwell Publishers, Oxford, 1994.

[FIS 96] FISHER M.M., SCHOLTEN H.J., UNWIN D., "Geographic information systems, spatial data analysis and spatial modelling", in FISCHER M.M., SCHOLTEN H.J., UNWIN D. (eds), *Spatial Analytical Perspectives on GIS*, Taylor and Francis, London, pp. 3–19, 1996.

[FOG 10] FOGG B.J., Thoughts on persuasive technology, [en ligne], available at: captology.stanford.edu/resources/thoughts-on-persuasive-technology.html, 2010.

[FLO 10] FLORIDI L., "Preface", in FLORIDI L. (ed.), *The Cambridge Handbook of Information and Computer Ethics*, Cambridge University Press, pp. 9–15, 2010.

[FRI 70] FRIEDMAN M., "The social responsibility of business is to increase its profits", *New York Times*, vol. 32, no. 13, pp. 122–126, 1970.

[FRI 02] FRIEDMAN B., KAHN P.H., BORNING A., Value sensitive design: theory and methods, University of Washington, Dept. of Computer Science & Eng., Technical Report, 02 December 2001, 2002.

[FRO 95] FROLICK M.N., ROBICHAUX B.P., "EIS information requirements determination: using a group support system to enhance the strategic business objectives method", *Decision Support Systems*, vol. 14, no. 2, pp. 157–170, 1995.

[FUX 04] FUXMAN A., LIU L., PISTORE M. *et al.*, "Specifying and analyzing early requirements in tropos", *Requirements Engineering Journal*, vol. 9, no. 2, pp. 132–150, 2004.

[GAB 98] GABB A.P., "The requirement spectrum", *Proceedings of the 1st Symposium of the Systems Engineering Society of Australia, INCOSE Region 6*, 1998.

[GAC 05] GACHET A., SPRAGUE R., "A context-based approach to the development of decision support systems", *Proceedings of the 5th International and Interdisciplinary Conference on Modeling and Using Context*, Paris, France, 5–8 July 2005.

[GAM 08] GAM I., Ingénierie des Exigences pour les Systèmes d'Information Décisionnels: Concepts, Modèles et Processus, PhD Thesis, University of Paris I-Panthéon-Sorbonne, 2008.

[GAR 12] GARTNER, Gartner says worldwide business intelligence, analytics and performance management software market surpassed the $12 billion mark in 2011, available at: www.gartner.com/newsroom/id/1971516, 2012.

[GIO 08] GIORGINI P., RIZZI S., GARZETTI M., "GRAnD: a goal-oriented approach to requirement analysis in data warehouses", *Decision Support Systems*, vol. 45, pp. 4–21, 2008.

[GIR 83] GIRIN J., Les machines de gestion [Management machines], report by the CRG (Centre de Recherches en Gestion), École Polytechnique, 1983.

[GOL 09] GOLFARELLI M., "From user requirements to conceptual design in data warehouse design – a survey", in BELLATRECHE L. (ed.), *Data Warehousing Design and Advanced Engineering Applications: Methods for Complex Construction*, IGI Global, pp. 1–14, 2009.

[GOR 71] GORRY G.A., SCOTT MORTON M., "A framework for management information systems", *Sloan Management Review*, vol. 13, no. 1, pp. 50–70, 1971.

[GOT 91] GOTTERBARN D., "Ethical considerations in software engineering", *Proceedings of the 13th International Conference on Software Engineering*, IEEE Press, pp. 266–274, 1991.

[GRI 13] GRINBERG N., NAAMAN M., SHAW B. et al., "Extracting diurnal patterns of real world activity from social media", *Proceedings of the 7th International AAAI Conference on Weblogs and Social Med (ICWSM'13)*, Boston, July 2013.

[GUI 71] GUIBERT B., LAGANIER J., VOLLE M., "Essai sur les nomenclatures industrielles", *Économie et Statistique*, no. 20, pp. 23–36, February 1971.

[GUO 06] Guo Y., Tang S., Tong Y. *et al.*, "Triple-driven data modeling methodology in data warehousing: a case study", *Proceedings of ACM International Workshop on Data Warehousing and OLAP (DOLAP)*, pp. 59–66, 2006.

[HAB 99] Habermas J., "A genealogical analysis of the cognitive content of morality", in Habermas J., *The Inclusion of the Other*, Polity Press, Cambridge, pp. 3–48, 1999.

[HAC 06] Hacking I., Cours "B": Les choses, les gens et la raison, Collège de France, May 2006.

[HAN 12] Hanachi C., Charoy F., Stinckwich S., "Introduction to the collaborative technology for coordinating crisis management (CT2CM) track", *IEEE 21st International Workshop on Enabling Technologies: Infrastructure for Collaborative Enterprises*, pp. 349–351, 2012.

[HEL 96] Herlea D.E., "Users' involvement in the requirements engineering process", *Proceedings of the 10th Knowledge Acquisition for Knowledge-Based Systems Workshop (KAW 96)*, 1996.

[HOF 92] Hofstede G.J., Modesty in Modelling: on the Application of Interactive Planning Systems, with a Case Study in Pot Plant Cultivation, Thesis Publisher, Amsterdam, 1992.

[HOO 08] Hood C., Wiedemann S., Fichtinger S. *et al.*, *Requirements Management. The Interface Between Requirements Development and all Other Systems Engineering Processes*, Springer, Berlin Heidelberg, 2008.

[HOR 14] Horkoff J., Barone D., Jiang L. *et al.*, "Strategic business modeling: representation and reasoning", *Software and System Modeling*, vol. 13, no. 2, pp. 1015–1041, 2014.

[HOS 07] Hosack B., "The effect of system feedback and decision context on value-based decision-making behavior", *Decision Support Systems*, vol. 43, pp. 1605–1614, 2007.

[HOS 14] Hosack B., Paradice D., "Increasing personal value congruence in computerized decision support using system feedback", *Axioms*, vol. 3, pp. 84–108, 2014.

[IBM 09] IBM, available at: http://www.ibm.com/developerworks/patterns/bi/concepts.html, 2009.

[JOH 85] Johnson D., *Computer Ethics*, 1st ed., Prentice-Hall, Englewood Cliffs, 1985.

[JON 79] JONAS H., *Das Prinzip Verantwortung. Versuch einer Ethik für die technologische Zivilisation*, Insel Verlag, Frankfurt a. M., 1979.

[KAN 91] KANT, *The Metaphysics of Morals*, First published 1797, Translated by GREGOR M.J., Cambridge University Press, 1991

[KAP 96] KAPLAN R.S., NORTON D.P., *Balanced Scorecard, Translating Strategy into Action*, Harvard Business School Press, 1996.

[KAS 93] KAST R., *La théorie de la décision*, La Découverte, Paris, 1993.

[KEE 78] KEEN P., SCOTT MORTON M., *Decision Support Systems: an Organizational Perspective*, Addison-Wesley Publishing, Reading, MA, 1978.

[KEE 87] KEEN P., "Decision support systems: the next decade", *Decision Support Systems*, vol. 3, no. 3, pp. 253–265, 1987.

[KLA 07] KLASHNER R., SABET S., "A DSS design model for complex problems: lessons from mission critical infrastructure", *Decision Support Systems*, vol. 43, no. 3, pp. 990–1013, April 2007.

[KOU 06] KOUROUTHANASSIS P.E., GIAGLIS G.M., "A design theory for pervasive systems", *International Workshop on Ubiquitous Computing (IWUC)*, pp. 62–70, 2006.

[KRA 14] KRASNOW WATERMAN K., BRUENING P., "Big Data analytics: risks and responsibilities", *International Data Privacy Law*, vol. 4, no. 2, pp. 89–95, 2014.

[LAP 05] LAPOUCHNIAN A., Goal-oriented requirements engineering: an overview of the current research, Technical Report, University of Toronto, 2005.

[LAS 05] LASCOUMES P., LE GALÈS P., "Conclusion", in LASCOUMES P., LE GALÈS P. (eds), *Gouverner par les instruments*, Presses de Sciences Po Académique, Paris, pp. 357–370, 2005.

[LAZ 14] LAZER D., KENNEDY R., KING G. *et al.*, Google flu trends still appears sick: an evaluation of the 2013-2014 flu season, SSRN Scholarly Paper, Social Science Research Network, Rochester, NY, 2014.

[LEG 05] LE GALÈS P., "Contrôle et surveillance: la restructuration de l'État en Grande-Bretagne", in LASCOUMES P., LE GALÈS P. (eds), *Gouverner par les instruments*, Presses de Sciences Po Académique, Paris, pp. 237–271, 2005.

[LEM 73] LE MOIGNE J.-L., *Les systèmes d'information dans les organisations*, Presses Universitaires de France, Paris, 1973.

[LEM 77] LE MOIGNE J.-L., *La théorie du système général. Théorie de la modélisation*, Presses Universitaires de France, Paris, 1977.

[LEM 91] LE MOIGNE J.-L., "La conception des systèmes d'information organisationnels: de l'ingénierie informatique à l'ingénierie des systèmes", *Colloque AFCET: Autour et à l'entour de Merise, les méthodes de conception en perspective*, Sophia Antipolis, 17–19 April 1991.

[LÉV 89] LÉVINE P., POMEROL J.-CH., *Systèmes interactifs d'aide à la décision et systèmes experts*, Hermès, Paris, 1989.

[LEW 47] LEWIN K., "Frontiers in group dynamics: I. concept, method and reality in social science, social equilibria and social change", *Human Relation*, vol. 1, no. 1, pp. 5–41, 1947.

[LIS 00] LIST B., SCHIEFER J., TJOA A.M., "Process-oriented requirement analysis supporting the data warehouse design process – a use case driven approach", *Database and Expert Systems Applications*, Lecture Notes in Computer Science, vol. 1873, pp. 593–603, 2000.

[LIS 02] LIST B., BRUCKNER R.M., MACHACZEK K. *et al.*, "A comparison of data warehouse development methodologies case study of the process warehouse", *Proceedings of DEXA'2002*, pp. 203–215, 2002.

[LOR 05] LORRAIN D., "Les pilotes invisibles de l'action publique. Le désarroi du politique?", in LASCOUMES P., LE GALÈS P. (eds), *Gouverner par les instruments*, Presses de Sciences Po Académique, Paris, pp. 163–197, 2005.

[MAR 91] MARTIN J., *Rapid Application Development*, Macmillan Publishing Company, New York, 1991.

[MAR 01] MARAKAS G.M., *Systems Analysis and Design an Active Approach*, Prentice Hall, Upper Saddle River, 2001.

[MAR 03] MARAKAS G.M., *Decision Support Systems in the Twenty-First Century*, 2nd ed., Prentice Hall, Upper Saddle River, 2003.

[MAS 86] MASON R.O., "Four Ethical Issues of the Information Age", *MIS Quarterly*, vol. 10, no. 1, pp. 4–12, 1986.

[MAT 07a] MATHIESON K., "Towards a design science of ethical decision support", *Journal of Business Ethics*, vol. 76, pp. 269–292, 2007.

[MAT 07b] MATHIESON K., "Dioptra: an ethics decision support system", *Paper presented at the Americas Conference on Computer Information Systems*, Keystone, Colorado, 2007.

[MAY 13] MAYER-SCHONBERGER V., CUKIER K., *Big Data: a Revolution that will Transform How We Live, Work, and Think*, John Murray Publishers Ltd, 2013.

[MÉL 72] MÉLÈSE J., *L'analyse modulaire des systèmes de gestion*, Éditions Hommes et Techniques, Puteaux, 1972.

[MÉL 79] MÉLÈSE J., *Approches systémiques des organisations*, Éditions Hommes et Techniques, Puteaux, 1979.

[MER 03] MEREDITH R., ARNOTT D., "On ethics and decision support systems development", *7th Pacific Asia Conference on Information Systems*, Adelaide, South Australia, pp. 1562–1575, 10–13 July, 2003.

[MES 12] MESSERLI F.H., "Chocolate consumption, cognitive function, and nobel laureates", *New England Journal of Medicine*, vol. 367, no. 16, pp. 1562–1564, 18 October 2012.

[MET 10] METZGER J.-L., "Peut-on sortir de la crise sans re-penser la gestion?", *Savoir agir*, no. 13, pp. 39–47, 2010.

[MIN 76] MINTZBERG H., RAISINGHANI D., THÉORÊT A., "The structure of 'unstructured' decision processes", *Administrative Science Quarterly*, vol. 21, no. 2, pp. 246–275, June 1976.

[MIN 94] MINTZBERG H., *The Rise and Fall of Strategic Planning*, The Free Press, New York, 1994.

[MIN 10] MINGERS J., WALSHAM G., "Towards ethical information systems: the contribution of discourse ethics", *MIS Quarterly*, vol. 34, no. 4, pp. 833–854, 2010.

[MIT 93] MITROFF I.I., LINSTONE H.A., *The Unbounded Mind: Breaking the Chains of Traditional Business Thinking*, Oxford University Press, New York, 1993.

[MIT 97] MITROFF I.I., *Smart Thinking for Crazy Times. The Art of Solving the Right Problems*, Berret Koehler Publishers, San Francisco, 1997.

[MIT 10] MITROFF I.I., SILVERS A., *Dirty Rotten Strategies: How We Trick Ourselves and Others into Solving the Wrong Problems Precisely*, Stanford University Press, Stanford, CA, 2010.

[MOA 08] MOATI PH., *L'économie des bouquets*, Éditions de l'Aube, 2008.

[MOO 85] MOOR J.H., "What is computer ethics?", *Metaphilosophy*, vol. 16, no. 4, pp. 266–275, 1985.

[MOW 76] MOWSHOWITZ A., *The Conquest of Will: Information Processing in Human Affairs*, Addison-Wesley, Reading, 1976.

[MUC 13] MUCCHIELLI R., *La dynamique des groupes*, 22nd ed., ESF Éditeur, 2013.

[MYL 99] MYLOPOULOS J., CHUNG L., YU E., "From object-oriented to goal-oriented requirements analysis", *Communications of the ACM*, vol. 42, no. 1, pp. 31–37, 1999.

[MYL 00] MYLOPOULOS J., "Desert island column: a trip to Carthea", *Automated Software Engineering*, vol. 7, no. 4, pp. 377–380, 2000.

[NEB 12] NEBOT V., BERLANGA R., "Building data warehouses with semantic web data", *Decision Support Systems*, vol. 52, no. 4, pp. 853–868, March 2012.

[NEU 00] NEUMAN W.L., *Social Research Methods: Qualitative and Quantitative Approaches*, 4th ed., Allyn and Bacon, Needham Heights, MA, 2000.

[NIS 98] NISSENBAUM H., "Values in the design of computer systems", *Computers and Society*, pp. 38–39, March 1998.

[NYL 99] NYLUND A., "Tracing the BI family tree", *Knowledge Management*, CurtCo Freedom Group, pp. 70–71, July 1999.

[PAR 08] PARADICE D., "Decision support and problem formulation activity", in ADAM F., HUMPHREYS P. (eds) *Encyclopedia of Decision Making and Decision Support Technologies*, IGI Global, pp. 192–199, 2008.

[PAU 01] PAULRÉ B., "Le capitalisme cognitif, un nouveau programme de recherche", in DIEUAIDE P., CORSANI A., AZAÏS CH. (eds), *Vers un capitalisme cognitif: entre mutations du travail et territoires*, L'Harmattan, pp. 7–21, 2001.

[PEA 95] PEARSON J.M., SHIM J.P., "An empirical investigation into DSS structures and environments", *Decision Support Systems*, vol. 13, pp. 141–158, 1995.

[PER 04] PERINI A., SUSI A., "Developing a decision support system for integrated production in agriculture", *Environmental Modelling and Software Journal*, vol. 19, no. 9, 2004.

[POH 10] POHL K., *Requirements Engineering – Fundamentals, Principles, and Techniques*, Springer Verlag, 2010.

[POM 05] POMEROL J.-C., ADAM F., "On the legacy of Herbert Simon and his contribution to decision making support systems and artificial intelligence," in GUPTA J., FORGIONNNE G., MORA M. (eds), *Intelligent Decision-Making Support Systems (i-DMSS): Foundations, Applications and Challenges*, Springer Verlag, London, pp. 25–43, 2005.

[POR 85] PORTER M., *Competitive Advantage*, Free Press, New York, 1985.

[POW 01] POWER D.J., "Supporting decision-makers: an expanded framework", *Conference: Informing Science Challenges to Informing Clients. A Transdisciplinary Approach*, Krakow, Poland, pp. 431–436, 2001.

[POW 04] POWER D.J., Decision support systems web tour, version 4.3., available at http://dssresources.com. 2004.

[POW 07] POWER D.J., A brief history of decision support systems, available at http://DSSResources.com/history/dsshistory.html, version 4.0, 10 March 2007.

[POW 09] POWER D.J., *Decision Support Basics*, Business Expert Press, New York, 2009.

[PRA 97] PRAT N., "Goal formalisation and classification for requirements engineering", in DUBOIS E., OPDAHL A.L., POHL K. (eds), *Proceedings of the 3rd International Workshop on Requirements Engineering: Foundations of Software Quality (REFSQ'97)*, Presses Universitaires de Namur, pp. 145–156, 1997.

[PRU 14] PRUD'HOMME B., GOMPEL N., "Quand Google rencontre Descartes", *Le Monde*, 8 October 2014.

[RAI 68] RAIFFA H., *Decision Analysis*, Addison-Wesley, Reading, 1968.

[RAS 04] RASTIER F., Doxa et lexique en corpus – pour une sémantique des idéologies, *Texto!*, December, available at http://www.revue-texto.net/ Inedits/Rastier /Rastier_Doxa.html, 2004.

[RAS 06] RASTIER F., "De la signification lexicale au sens textuel : éléments pour une approche unifiée", *Texto!*, vol. XI, no. 1, 2006.

[RAV 07] RAVAT F., Modèles et outils pour la conception et la manipulation de systèmes d'aide à la décision, Habilitation à diriger des recherches, University of Toulouse I, 2007.

[REG 03] REGEV G., A systemic paradigm for early IT system requirements based on regulation principles, PhD Thesis, École Polytechnique Fédérale de Lausanne, 2003.

[REI 02] REIX R., ROWE F., "La recherche en système d'information: de l'histoire au concept", in ROWE F. (ed.), *Faire de la recherche en systèmes d'information*, Vuibert, Paris, pp. 1–17, 2002.

[RIC 98] RICŒUR P., "Éthique", *Encyclopædia Universalis*, 1998.

[RIC 00] RICŒUR P., "De la morale à l'éthique et aux éthiques", in APPEL K.-O. (ed.), *Un siècle de philosophie 1900-2000*, Gallimard, Paris, pp.103–120, 2000.

[RIT 73] RITTEL H.W.J., WEBBER M.M., "Dilemmas in a general theory of planning", *Policy Sciences*, vol. 4, pp. 155–169, 1973.

[RIT 05] RITCHEY T., Wicked problems: structuring social messes with morphological analysis, Swedish Morphological Society, available at: www.swemorph.com, 2005.

[ROC 79] ROCKART J.F., "Chief executives define their own data needs", *Harvard Business Review*, vol. 57, no. 2, pp. 81–93, March–April 1979.

[ROG 00] ROGERSON S., WECKERT J., SIMPSON C., "An ethical review of information systems development: the Australian Computer Society's Code of Ethics and SSADM", *Information Technology and People*, vol. 13, no. 2, pp. 121–136, 2000.

[ROL 99] ROLLAND C., PRAKASH N., From conceptual modelling to requirements engineering, CREWS Report series 99–11, 1999.

[ROL 11] ROLLAND C., "De la modélisation conceptuelle à l'ingénierie des exigences", *Techniques de l'ingénieur*, ref. H3250, 10 February 2011.

[ROS 77] ROSS D.T., SCHOMAN K.E. Jr, "Structured analysis for requirements definition", *IEEE Transactions on Software Engineering*, vol. SE-3, no. 1, pp. 6–15, 1977.

[ROS 08] ROSENTHAL-SABROUX C., GRUNDSTEIN M., "A knowledge management approach of ICT", *VNU Journal of Science, Natural Sciences and Technology*, no. 24, pp. 162–169, 2008.

[ROU 14] ROUVROY A., "De la gouvernementalité algorithmique de fait au nouvel état de droit qu'il lui faut", *Notes du Séminaire Digital Studies*, Paris, 7 October 2014.

[ROW 09] ROWE F., "Les approches critiques en Systèmes d'Information: de la sociologie de la domination à l'éthique de l'émancipation", *Économies .et Sociétés*, no. 12, pp. 2081–2114, 2009.

[SAL 04] SALAIS R., "La politique des indicateurs. Du taux de chômage au taux d'emploi dans la stratégie européenne pour l'emploi", in ZIMMERMANN B. (ed.), *Les sciences sociales à l'épreuve de l'action*, Éditions de la MSH, collection du CIERA "Dialogiques", pp. 287–331, 2004.

[SAL 06] SALLES M., *Stratégies des PME et intelligence économique. Une méthode d'analyse du besoin*, 2nd ed., Économica, Paris, 2006.

[SAL 07a] SALLES M., "Présentation du dossier 'Représentations, modèles et normes pour l'entreprise'", in SALLES M. (ed.), *Représentations, modèles et normes pour l'entreprise, Revue Droit et Société*, no. 65, pp. 21–26, 2007.

[SAL 07b] SALLES M., COLLETIS G., "Représentations de l'entreprise dans les systèmes d'information statistique et décision dans les collectivités territoriales", in SALLES M. (ed.), *Représentations, modèles et normes pour l'entreprise, Revue Droit et Société*, no. 65, pp. 53–74, 2007.

[SAL 09] SALLAM R.L., SCHLEGEL K., "Overcoming the gap between business intelligence and decision support", *Gartner*, ID: G00165169, 9 April 2009.

[SAL 10] SALLES M., "Supporting public decision making – a progressive approach aided by an ontology", *International Journal of Decision Support System Technology*, special issue: Semantic Decision Support Systems, vol. 2, no. 1, pp. 21–36, 2010.

[SAL 13a] SALLES M., Ingénierie de méthodes d'ingénierie des exigences pour l'aide à la décision, Habilitation à diriger des recherches, University of Toulouse I-Capitole/IRIT, 2013.

[SAL 13b] SALLES M., COLLETIS G., "Déconstruire la doxa dominante, construire une pensée politique alternative. Du lien entre les représentations, les principes et les normes", *LoSguardo*, The Instruments of the Power: from the Prince to Archaeologist, XIII, 10, pp. 391–414, 2013.

[SAL 15] SALLES M., "La responsabilité économique et sociale des concepteurs de systèmes d'information: contribution à une éthique appliquée", *Innovations. Revue d'Économie et de Management de l'Innovation (I-REMI)*, vol. 4, no. 46, pp. 197–226, 2015.

[SAN 12] SANDEL M., *What Money Can't Buy*, Macmillan, 2012.

[SCT 03] SCT (Secrétariat du Conseil du Trésor), Guide sur les indicateurs, Québec, 2003.

[SEL 89] SELIGMANN P.S., WIJERS G.M., SOL H.G., "Analysing the structure of I.S. methodologies, an alternative approach", *Proceedings of the 1st Dutch Conference in Information Systems*, Amersfoort, The Netherlands, 1989.

[SHI 02] SHIM J.P., WARKENTIN M., COURTNEY J.F. *et al.*, "Past, present, and future of decision support technology", *Decision Support Systems*, vol. 33, pp. 111–126, 2002.

[SIM 56] SIMON H.A., "Rational choice and the structure of the environment", *Psychological Review*, vol. 63, no. 2, pp. 129–138, 1956.

[SIM 60] SIMON H.A., *The New Science of Management Decision*, Harper & Row Publishers, New York, 1960.

[SIM 76] SIMON H.A., "From substantive to procedural rationality", in LATSIS S.J. (ed.), *Method and Appraisal in Economics*, Cambridge University Press, Cambridge, pp. 129–148, 1976.

[SIM 77] SIMON H.A., *The New Science of Management Decision* (3rd revised edition), Prentice-Hall, New Jersey, 1977.

[SIM 78] SIMON H.A., "Rationality as process and as product of a thought", *American Economic Review,* vol. 68, no. 2, pp. 1–16, 1978.

[SIM 79] SIMON H.A., *Models of Thought*, Yale University Press, New Haven, 1979.

[SIM 86] SIMON H.A., DANTZIG G.B., HOGARTH R. *et al.*, Research Briefings 1986: Report of the Research Briefing Panel on Decision Making and Problem Solving, National Academy Press, Washington, DC, 1986.

[SIM 97] SIMON H.A., *Administrative Behavior* (4th expanded ed.; 1st ed. 1947), The Free Press, New York, 1997.

[SMI 99] SMITH J., HASNAS J., "Ethics and information systems: the corporate domain", *MIS Quarterly*, vol. 23, no. 1, pp. 109–127, 1999.

[SPR 80] SPRAGUE R.H. Jr., "A framework for the development of decision support systems", *MIS Quarterly*, vol. 4, no. 4, pp. 1–26, December 1980.

[SPR 82] SPRAGUE R.H. Jr., CARLSON E.D., *Building Effective Decision Support Systems*, Prentice-Hall, 1982.

[STA 08a] STAHL B.C., "Researching ethics and morality in information systems: some guiding questions", International Conference on Information Systems (*ICIS 2008*), pp. 1–17, 2008.

[STA 08b] STAHL B.C., "Ethical issues of information and business", in HIMMA K.E., TAVANI H.T. (eds), *The Handbook of Information and Computer Ethics*, John Wiley & Sons, pp. 311–335, 2008.

[STA 10] STAHL B.C., "Social issues in computer ethics", in FLORIDI L. (ed.), *The Cambridge Handbook of Information and Computer Ethics*, Cambridge University Press, pp. 101–115, 2010.

[STI 14] STIEGLER B., "De la gouvernementalité algorithmique de fait au nouvel état de droit qu'il lui faut", *Notes du Séminaire Digital Studies*, Paris, 7 October 2014.

[SUN 01] SUN L., LIU K., "A method for interactive articulation of information requirements for strategic decision support", *Information and Software Technology*, vol. 43, no. 4, pp. 247–263, March 2001.

[TIF 13] TIFFON G., *La mise au travail des clients*, Economica, coll. "Études sociologiques", 2013.

[TIM 94] TIMPKA T., JOHANSSON M., "The need for requirements engineering in the development of clinical decision-support systems: a qualitative study", *Methods of Information in Medicine*, vol. 33, no. 2, pp. 227–33, 1994.

[TUR 95] TURBAN E., *Decision Support and Expert Systems: Management Support Systems*, Maxwell McMillan, New York, 1995.

[VAN 00] VAN LAMSWEERDE A., "Requirements engineering in the year 00: a research perspective", *Proceeding of the 22nd International Conference on Software Engineering*, ACM Press, pp. 5–19, 2000.

[VAN 01] VAN LAMSWEERDE A., "Goal-oriented requirements engineering: a guided tour", *Proceedings of the 5th IEEE International Symposium on Requirements Engineering (RE'01)*, Toronto, pp. 249–263, 2001.

[VAN 08] VAN DEN HOVEN J., "Moral methodology and information technology", in HIMMA K.E., TAVANI H.T. (eds), *The Handbook of Information and Computer Ethics*, John Wiley & Sons, pp. 49–67, 2008.

[VAN 09] VAN LAMSWEERDE A., *Requirements Engineering: from System Goals to UML Models to Software Specifications*, John Wiley and Sons, 2009.

[VOL 91] VOLONINO L., WATSON H.J., "The strategic business objectives method for guiding executive information systems development", *Journal of Management Information Systems*, vol. 7, no. 3, pp. 27–39, Winter 1991.

[WAL 93] WALSHAM G., "Ethical issues in information systems development", *The IFIP 8.2 Working Group Information Systems Development: Human, Social and Organizational Aspects*, North-Holland, Noordwijkerhout, The Netherlands, 1993.

[WAL 11] WALSHAM G., *Interpreting Information Systems in Organizations*, available at http://dl.dropbox.com/u/31779972/Interpreting%20Information%20Systems%20in%20Organizations.pdf, 2011.

[WAT 89] WATSON H.J., GLOVER H., "Common and avoidable causes of EIS failure", *Computerworld*, vol. 4, pp. 90–91, December 1989.

[WEI 76] WEIZENBAUM J., *Computer Power and Human Reason: from Judgment to Calculation*, W. H. Freeman, San Francisco, 1976.

[WIE 48] WIENER N., *Cybernetics or Control and Communication in the Animal and the Machine*, MIT Press, Cambridge, 1948.

[WIE 89] WIENER N., *The Human Use of Human Beings. Cybernetics and Society*, London: Free association books, First published in 1950 and revised in 1954, Houghton Mifflin, 1989.

[WIN 03] WINTER R., STRAUCH B., "A method for demand-driven information requirements analysis in data warehousing projects", *Proceedings 36th Hawaii International Conference on System Sciences (HICSS)*, Hawaii, pp. 1359–1365, 2003.

[YU 94] YU E.S.K., Modelling strategic relationships for process reengineering, PhD Thesis, University of Toronto, Canada, 1994.

[ZHU 13] ZHUANG Z.Y., WILKIN C.L., CEGLOWSKI A., "A framework for an intelligent decision support system: a case in pathology test ordering", *Decision Support Systems*, vol. 55, no. 2, pp. 476–487, May 2013.

Index

Other titles from

in

Information Systems, Web and Pervasive Computing

STOCKINGER Peter
Introduction to Audiovisual Archives

STOCKINGER Peter
Digital Audiovisual Archives

VENTRE Daniel
Cyberwar and Information Warfare

2010

BONNET Pierre
Enterprise Data Governance

BRUNET Roger
Sustainable Geography

CARREGA Pierre
Geographical Information and Climatology

CAUVIN Colette, ESCOBAR Francisco, SERRADJ Aziz
Thematic Cartography – 3-volume series
Thematic Cartography and Transformations – volume 1
Cartography and the Impact of the Quantitative Revolution – volume 2
New Approaches in Thematic Cartography – volume 3

LANGLOIS Patrice
Simulation of Complex Systems in GIS

MATHIS Philippe
Graphs and Networks – 2nd edition

THÉRIAULT Marius, DES ROSIERS François
Modeling Urban Dynamics

2009

BONNET Pierre, DETAVERNIER Jean-Michel, VAUQUIER Dominique
Sustainable IT Architecture: the Progressive Way of Overhauling
Information Systems with SOA

PAPY Fabrice
Information Science

RIVARD François, ABOU HARB Georges, MERET Philippe
The Transverse Information System

ROCHE Stéphane, CARON Claude
Organizational Facets of GIS

VENTRE Daniel
Information Warfare

2008

BRUGNOT Gérard
Spatial Management of Risks

FINKE Gerd
Operations Research and Networks

GUERMOND Yves
Modeling Process in Geography

KANEVSKI Michael
Advanced Mapping of Environmental Data

MANOUVRIER Bernard, LAURENT Ménard
Application Integration: EAI, B2B, BPM and SOA

PAPY Fabrice
Digital Libraries

2007

DOBESCH Hartwig, DUMOLARD Pierre, DYRAS Izabela
Spatial Interpolation for Climate Data

SANDERS Lena
Models in Spatial Analysis

2006

CLIQUET Gérard
Geomarketing

CORNIOU Jean-Pierre
Looking Back and Going Forward in IT

DEVILLERS Rodolphe, JEANSOULIN Robert
Fundamentals of Spatial Data Quality

Printed in the United States
By Bookmasters